TO RAISE THE FALLEN

To Raise the Fallen

A Selection of the War Letters,
Prayers and Spiritual Writings
of Fr Willie Doyle SJ

Compiled and edited by Patrick Kenny

VERITAS

282.415

Published 2017 by
Veritas Publications
7-8 Lower Abbey Street, Dublin 1, Ireland

publications@veritas.ie
www.veritas.ie

ISBN 978-1-84730-807-8

10 9 8 7 6 5 4 3 2 1

A catalogue record for this book is available from the British
Library.

Designed by Lir Mac Cárthaigh
Printed in Ireland by Watermans Printers Ltd, Cork

*Veritas books are printed on paper made from the wood pulp of managed
forests. For every tree felled, at least one tree is planted, thereby renewing
natural resources.*

Contents

Acknowledgements

A number of individuals have assisted with this work. Damien Burke of the Irish Jesuit Archives provided much kind assistance with sources, and shared his vast knowledge of Fr Doyle's writings and letters. Fr Bruce Bradley SJ and Fr John Hogan from the Diocese of Meath have provided important advice on particular aspects of the text. The Poor Clares in Cork kindly provided some letters, and the Missionaries of Charity provided helpful clarifications about Mother Teresa's adoption of some of Fr Doyle's spiritual practices. More generally, Fr Bernard McGuckian SJ has been a source of advice and inspiration relating to Fr Doyle over several years, and Carole Hope's correspondence and work has deepened my own knowledge of Fr Doyle's war service. Special thanks also to my family – Rachel, Marian, Lucia, Gemma and Teresa – for their support and patience.

More information about Fr Doyle can be found on www.fatherdoyle.com which is updated every day with quotes from Fr Doyle's writings. The following publications also provide important details about Fr Doyle's life:

Fr William Doyle SJ: A Spiritual Study by Alfred O'Rahilly (multiple editions from 1920s and 1930s) and *Merry in God* (1939) by Fr Charles Doyle SJ are both detailed accounts of all aspects of Willie Doyle's life. However, both books are out of print but can be found in many second-hand bookshops. *Worshipper and Worshipped* (2013) by Carole Hope is a definitive and detailed record of Willie Doyle's service as military chaplain.

Patrick Kenny
June 2017

Introduction

In May 1893, an unknown Irish Jesuit novice, using the devotional language of the era, wrote the following 'contract' in his private diary:

> Darling Mother Mary, in preparation for the glorious martyrdom which I feel assured thou art going to obtain for me, I, thy most unworthy child, on this the first day of thy month, solemnly commence my life of slow martyrdom by earnest hard work and constant self-denial. With my blood I promise thee to keep this resolution, do thou, sweet Mother, assist me and obtain for me the one favour I wish and long for: to die a Jesuit Martyr.

For twenty-four years, the young novice kept his promise to live a life of hard work and self-denial, and his wish was fulfilled: Fr Willie Doyle SJ died as a 'martyr of charity', struck by a German shell when he ran into no man's land to rescue two wounded soldiers on 16 August 1917.

* * *

William Joseph Gabriel Doyle, the youngest of seven children, was born on 3 March 1873 into a relatively comfortable Victorian home in Dalkey, a leafy seaside suburb on Dublin's southside. His father, Hugh, was a clerk of the High Court in Dublin and retired at the age of ninety, following a career spanning a remarkable seventy-three years. His youngest son seems to have inherited his prodigious work ethic.

Four of the seven children pursued religious vocations. One brother, Fred, initially entered the Jesuits before pursuing a vocation as a priest of the Dublin diocese; he sadly died of fever in Rome ten days before his ordination. His sister Mary become a Sister of Mercy and was based in Cobh, County Cork. Charlie, just a few years older than Willie, also became a Jesuit; the two were inseparable as youngsters and followed the same vocation in adulthood[1].

The family was deeply religious, and their devotion was given practical expression by their care for the less fortunate in the neighbourhood – long lines of the local poor visited the house at Christmas to receive financial assistance and gifts from the Doyle family. Very touchingly, young Charlie and Willie polished the coins they gave to the poor on these occasions, thus enhancing the dignity of the gift.

This spirit of practical charity seems to have profoundly shaped young Willie. He was a typical

1. Fr Charles Doyle SJ wrote *Merry in God*, a biography of Fr Willie, which was published in 1939. It was published anonymously at the time.

young boy in many respects – he loved sports, in particular swimming and cricket. From an early age he was fascinated with the military and loved playing soldiers, always insisting that he was fighting for Ireland. However, he was not typical when it came to his charity towards others. As a young boy he regularly helped the servants around the house, sometimes getting up early to light the fire or clean the dishes before they got up.

Fr Charles Doyle, writing about young Willie's childhood in *Merry in God*, describes his sacrifice of his first ever shilling:

He was quite a little fellow when he got his first shilling. A whole shilling! It seemed a fortune that would buy unlimited sweet things. In high glee he set out on a double errand, to visit a pastry shop at the corner of Dalkey Avenue, and an uncle who had recently returned from his travels. Half way down the avenue Willie met a beggar, and, as he often did, stopped to say a word to the poor man, who happened to have a long story that day. Willie's kind heart was touched with the tale of woe. Would not a shilling buy the bit of baccy, the ounce of tea, the many other necessities this poor old man had not? But the pastry shop was in sight, its windows filled with tempting cakes and sweets. There was a sharp struggle between nature and grace, but grace carried the day. The shilling passed from a hot little fist to the willing palm of the beggar, and Willie went his way with tears in his eyes; and as he said, describing the incident later, 'I howled all the way to uncle's'.

As he grew he developed a close relationship with his less fortunate neighbours, often squirrelling away food to give to them, or even cleaning and painting their houses when necessary. On one occasion, he encouraged a lonely dying neighbour to confess to a priest before death. The man refused, so the young Willie stayed with him for eight hours, praying and pleading until at last the man relented. He died soon after making his confession. This apostolic success was a preview of what was to come in his later life.

Young Willie was initially educated at home, and from the age of eleven to seventeen, he attended Ratcliffe College in Leicestershire, under the care of the Rosminians. He regularly won academic prizes, but he particularly excelled at sports, especially cricket and soccer. He returned home in delicate health in July 1890, and spent time in Dalkey considering his future.

Given his deep spirituality and dedication to the poor, it seemed an obvious choice for Willie to follow a vocation. His initial plan was to become a priest of the Dublin diocese to replace his late brother Fred. He had no interest in entering a religious order. As he told one of the Rosminian priests who taught him, 'I would as soon shoot myself as enter a religious order!'. However, this resolve was somewhat shaken on visiting his brother Charlie in the Jesuit novitiate in August 1890. His initial reaction to the idea of becoming a Jesuit was starkly negative, telling his brother that he 'would never come to this hole of a place!'. However, Charlie tried hard to recruit him, and gave him a booklet on the benefits of entering a religious order written by St Alphonsus de Liguori[2]. This book seems to have completely altered Willie's thinking, and by Christmas he had decided to become a Jesuit:

> I was alone in the drawing-room when father came in and asked me if I had yet made up my mind as to my future career. I answered 'yes' – that I intended to become a Jesuit. I remember how I played my joy and happiness into the piano after thus giving myself openly to Jesus.

Willie entered the Jesuit novitiate three months later, and his sixteen-years of formation were interspersed with periods spent at home due to ill health. He suffered with an unidentified digestive complaint for much of his life, including his time as a military chaplain. He also had a nervous breakdown which afflicted him after a fire broke out in the novitiate where he was living. He had to return home for a time, and there was a serious doubt as to whether

---

2.   *Instructions and Considerations on the Religious State.*

his health was robust enough for a religious vocation, with several doctors declaring him unfit for such a life. Nonetheless he persevered and his return to the novitiate was supported by the Provincial of the Jesuits. It was quite rare at the time that those with significant health problems of this sort were allowed to return to the novitiate. It's remarkable to consider how one who suffered so many health difficulties in his early years as a Jesuit was subsequently transformed into a rock of courage in the Great War.

Father Doyle was sent to Belgium and England to study philosophy, and was stationed in Milltown in Dublin for his theology studies. As a Jesuit scholastic he was also given appointments as a teacher and a prefect in both Belvedere College and Clongowes Wood College where he was instrumental in founding both the Clongownian and the Clongowes Union. He was ordained a priest on 28 July 1907, in the same ceremony as Blessed John Sullivan SJ[3].

---

3. John Sullivan was the son of the Lord Chancellor and was born in 1861. He was raised in the Church of Ireland. He studied classics, became a barrister and had a love of dining and fine clothes – he was known to some as the best dressed man in Dublin. To the surprise of many, he converted to Catholicism at the age of thirty-five. He entered the Jesuits four years later. Ordained at the age of forty-six, he spent most of his priesthood in Clongowes Wood College where he was especially known for his humility, care for the poor and sick, and for his apparent gifts of healing. He died aged seventy-one and devotion to him grew after his death, with many people claiming extraordinary

Most of his priesthood was spent on the Jesuit mission team, preaching missions in parishes and giving retreats to religious communities around Ireland. His impact seems to have been electrifying. To quote only one of many testimonies, one parish priest declared:

> The results of your mission have exceeded my anticipations and all previous experiences. Indeed the people speak of it with awe, as of a miraculous manifestation and veritable outpouring of grace.

In the words of Pope Francis, he often went to the 'peripheries' to seek those alienated from the Church. He visited them at home, and was known to wait on the docks for sailors arriving into port late at night or to go out to meet factory workers on their way to work at dawn. He seemed to have a special gift for connecting with disaffected or wounded souls. As he noted on one occasion:

> I have not met a single refusal to come to the mission or to confession so far during my missionary career. Why should there be one because Jesus for some mysterious reason seems to delight in using perhaps the most wretched of all his priests

favours through his intercession. He was beatified in Dublin on 13 May 2017.

as the channel of his grace? When I go to see a hard hopeless case, I cannot describe what happens exactly, but I seem to be able to lift up my heart like a cup and pour grace and the love of God upon that poor soul. I can see the result instantly, almost like the melting of snow.

One striking example of his effect on others occurred during his mission in Yarmouth in 1908:

I had a strange experience which seemed providential. In my wanderings through the slums I came across by accident an old woman over ninety who had not entered a church for long, long years. 'I have led a wicked life,' she said, 'but every day I asked God to send me a good friend before I died and I feel now my prayer is heard.' The next day I came back and heard her Confession, and brought her Holy Communion on Easter Sunday. As the tears streamed down her old withered face she said, 'Oh, Father this is the first happy day of my life, for I have never known what happiness is since I was a child.' I could not help feeling that the opening of heaven to that poor sinner was a reward more than enough for all the long years of preparation now passed.

He found retreats and missions to be personally taxing, and consequently was often tempted to give up the work. But he sought the inspiration and grace to proceed in a life of intense prayer – those who observed him in this work reported that he rarely seemed to sleep and spent many hours at night in prayer, but nonetheless remained full of energy and zeal.

He was particularly devoted to helping ordinary workingmen. At a time when holiness was often seen as the preserve of priests and nuns, he understood the importance of reaching ordinary lay people. He travelled across the continent to study the growing phenomenon of retreats for workers and wrote a booklet on the importance of this apostolate for Ireland. The idea of residential retreats for lay people seems commonplace to us now but it was a novelty one hundred years ago.

He tested his ideas for retreats with the employees of Providence Woollen Mills in County Mayo in April 1915. The workers were housed in a local school and looked after by the local Sisters of Charity. There was some initial scepticism from the workers about the prospect of such a retreat, but apparently all were won over in the end. According to one of the attendees:

No man ever made such an impression. Father Doyle's saintly appearance and attractive manner at once captured our attention, and time passed so quickly while he spoke that each lecture, though invariably half an hour, seemed but a moment. His words were simple and clear, and delivered in so kindly and gentle a fashion that they were just what he liked to call them – 'little chats'. We had been accustomed to fiery threatening sermons at missions, where God's justice is painted with so much eloquence, making one tremble at the uncertainty of salvation. But here the words of the saintly preacher sent us away with the impression: 'How easy it is after all for me to save my soul! God is good, he loves me, and what he asks is very small.'

His ultimate aim was to establish a permanent retreat house for workers. A building was identified by the Jesuits and Fr Doyle was to take charge of the entire project, but the building was burned down by suffragettes before it got off the ground! At that point the project was shelved for a period and it did not come to fruition until a retreat house for workers was finally opened in Rathfarnham Castle in Dublin four years after Fr Doyle's death.

But he did not confine his activities to retreats or missions and was highly sought after as a spiritual director, sometimes receiving several dozen letters per day seeking advice. He was instrumental in founding the Poor Clare convent in Cork; he raised large amounts of money for missions in Africa; helped establish an organisation for the spiritual support of priests and was also on the central council of the Pioneers. In fact, the founder of the Pioneers, Fr

James Cullen SJ, wanted him as his successor to lead the Pioneers, but a German shell sadly ended those plans.

It was perhaps his work for vocations that had the most lasting impact. He worked hard to encourage vocations to the priesthood and religious life. Convents were often full to overflowing in the early twentieth century and, when a place could not be found in Ireland, he helped young women to pursue their religious vocations in convents in other countries. This help was especially needed when there was a doubt about a girl's health, and he is known to have found American convents who would accept a girl with a wooden leg and another with a paralysed hand. He also established fundraising schemes to pay for the education of poor boys to the priesthood. Perhaps his greatest impact was with two bestselling pamphlets (*Vocations* and *Shall I be a Priest?*) that sold in their hundreds of thousands[4]. Excerpts from these publications can be found in chapter four.

In the midst of all this work, and indeed in the

---

4. I once received a letter from a priest in England who found his vocation after having read one of Fr Doyle's pamphlets. He was a veteran of World War II, and had been given the pamphlet by one of the army chaplains he met at that time. He met the chaplain again some years later and thanked him for the pamphlet and the impact it had on his life. The chaplain replied that he was the twelfth solider he personally knew who had become a priest after having read the pamphlet.

midst of his later life in the trenches, Fr Doyle retained his exuberant natural cheerfulness and the love of practical jokes. His optimistic and joyful approach to life was one of his most prominent and endearing characteristics. His brother Fr Charles Doyle recounts one early episode which occurred during Willie's novitiate while he was still a teenager, in which he utilised a dressed bolster as part of one of his pranks:

> Among the novices was a secular priest with whom Willie was very good friends but who was the object of many of his innocent pranks. One day during the summer vacation the novices were gathered outside the door of the novitiate, chatting and laughing, preparatory to moving off for a bathe. Willie, in hat and gown, appeared at an upper window. After exchanging some bantering remarks with his friend below, he withdrew. Suddenly there was a loud scream and a figure in hat and gown came hurtling through the air from the window where Willie had been a moment before … He rushed over, expecting to find Willie dead or badly injured, when Willie himself appeared at the window above, grinning and chuckling.

Father Doyle originally wanted to volunteer as a missionary in Africa. His notes from the retreat he made in 1907, not long after his ordination, give some indication of his motivations for wanting to pursue this path. He listed four arguments against offering himself for Africa (mostly focused on his desire to help Ireland), and thirteen arguments in favour of opting for the Congo mission, among which were the following:

- This thought has been in my mind for over twenty years and the thought of it has given me great pleasure and consolation
- My desire, even as a boy, to be a martyr
- The attraction I feel for a life of real privation and suffering
- The souls I shall be able to save

Father Doyle seriously prepared himself for the possibility of going to the mission in the Congo, and even took steps to learn the local language. However, for unknown reasons he was not chosen, and was instead appointed to the mission staff in Ireland.

However, the outbreak of World War I provided Fr Doyle with a unique missionary opportunity to satisfy his desire to help souls and also face the possibility of 'martyrdom' in the service of God and of others. Even in the trenches he was thinking of the Congo, and comparing it to life as a military chaplain:

You know my desire for the foreign missions because I realised that the privation and hardships of such a life, the separation from all naturally dear to me, would be an immense help to holiness. And here I am a real missioner, if not in the Congo, at least with many of the wants and sufferings and even greater dangers than I should have found there. The longing for martyrdom God has gratified times without number, for I have had to go into what seemed certain death, gladly making the offering of my poor life, but he did not accept it, so that the 'daily martyrdom' might be repeated.[5]

This letter, in addition to some of his other writings, provides a key insight into his motivation for volunteering for the front, namely the prospect of a 'hard' life that could help him grow in holiness, combined with a unique opportunity to be of service to souls in danger, which was probably all the more attractive as many of them were like the simple workers to whom he was so devoted. He was forever choosing the toughest road, for he felt that was his special calling, and the war was an opportunity not to be missed.

Father Doyle first volunteered as chaplain in November 1914. A few days after volunteering, his spiritual motivation for the offering was made explicit in his private diary:

5. Apparently the privations of the trenches did not dampen his zeal for the missionary life - he had also decided that, if he survived the war, he would volunteer to go and work in a leper colony.

My offering myself as war chaplain to the Provincial has had a wonderful effect on me. I long to go and shed my blood for Jesus, and, if he wills it, to die a martyr of charity. The thought that at any moment I may be called to the front, perhaps to die, has roused a great desire to do all I can while I have life. I feel great strength to make any sacrifice and little difficulty in doing so. I may not have long now to prove my love for Jesus.

Father Doyle had to wait a year until his offering of himself was accepted – he was appointed as chaplain in November 1915, travelling to join the 8th Battalion Royal Irish Fusiliers (part of the 16th [Irish] Division) in Surrey at the end of that month. As chaplain, Fr Doyle held the rank of captain, but despite the relative comforts he could have availed of, he was always to be found with his men, suffering along with them. As one Protestant officer noted:

Fr Doyle never rests. Night and day he is with us. He finds a dying or dead man, does all, comes back smiling, makes a little cross and goes out to bury him and then begins all over again.

The duties of a chaplain involved administering the sacraments, especially hearing confessions and giving the last rites, burying the dead and generally giving a morale boost to the troops. The powerful impact that

Fr Doyle's personality and presence had as a mission priest in Ireland was also evident in his dealings with the soldiers. To take just one of many examples, according to one non-Catholic soldier:

> Fr Doyle is a splendid fellow. He is so brave and cheery. He has a wonderful influence over others and can do what he likes with the men. I was out the other evening with a brother officer, and met him. After a few words I said: 'This is a pal of mine, Padre; he is a Protestant, but I think he would like your blessing'. Fr Doyle looked at my chum for a moment with a smile and then made the sign of the cross on his forehead. When he had passed on, my pal said: 'That is a holy man. Did you see the way he looked at me? It went right through me. And when he crossed my forehead I felt such an extraordinary sensation.'

Father Doyle was a dedicated letter writer and his correspondence with his father provides a valuable first-hand record of life in the trenches. These letters were, as he said on one occasion, written 'under all conditions and in all sorts of places, and sitting on a wet sandbag, with one's feet in four inches of mud, are not ideal conditions for composition'. Yet he persevered with the letters, even at the cost of his sleep, in order to bring solace to an elderly man in Dalkey who was evidently worried about his son. His deep love for his father is obvious in every letter, addressing him on practically every occasion as 'dearest father', and often signing off as 'your loving son, Willie'. Some extracts from Father Doyle's war letters, many of them truly moving, can be read in chapter one.

One specific form of suffering for Fr Doyle, as for all of the soldiers, was the discomfort of trench life. As Pope Francis would put it, he truly smelled of his sheep. Rats and other vermin were a particular annoyance. In one letter home he told his father that he had had:

> a good night's rest in spite of the hard floor and the friendly attention of one sweet little rat, a darling, with a long tail, who would persist in burrowing his way under my makeshift of a pillow. I am not exaggerating when I say the rats share our beds … I have serious fear for the end of my nose.

But surely the greatest crime the rats ever perpetrated on poor Fr Willie was to eat the pudding his sister sent to him during Christmas 1916![6]

Father Doyle's care for others cost him dearly at times. On one occasion, the medical doctor with whom he worked was sick, and there was no dry or warm spot for him to him to sleep in the dugout. Father Doyle lay face down on the ground to allow the doctor

---

6. See 'The tragic tale of the plum pudding' on p. 61 for the original letter extract.

to sleep on his back so that at least one of them could get some rest.

But the horrors of suffering, death and war did not alter his cheerful disposition, or his life-long love of practical jokes. Many of his letters contain a variety of interesting anecdotes and witticisms that suggest a joyful spirit in the midst of woe. To take just one example, he described a church in Amettes, France in the following terms:

> At the bottom of the same church is a mortuary slab, which reads as follows: Erected by Monsieur X in honour of his dear wife Marie who lived seventy-nine years, four months, six days. They were married fifty-five years, nine months, two days, seven hours. RIP. There is nothing like being accurate, but possibly this unfortunate man wanted to record that he had so much of his purgatory already done!

Father Doyle was present at several important battles, including the Battle of the Somme and the Battle of Messines Ridge, during which nearly one million pounds of explosives were detonated under the German trenches. The explosion, which at that that time was the largest ever created by man, could be heard as far away as London. His first-hand accounts of what he experienced during these and other major battles make for riveting reading. He was awarded the 16th (Irish) Division Parchment of Merit for bravery during a gas attack in April 1916, awarded the Military Cross for his bravery at the Somme, and nominated for both the Distinguished Service Order and Victoria Cross, neither of which were granted to him. There is some controversy surrounding the refusal of the Victoria Cross, with some suggestion that his Catholicism, and the fact that he was a Jesuit priest, were barriers to his receiving this award. Whatever the truth of this, it wouldn't bother Fr Doyle. He was very blasé about his Military Cross, and his only interest in it was the fact that it would make his beloved father proud:

> I am sorry these rewards are given to chaplains, for surely he would be a poor specimen of the Lord's anointed who would do his work for such a thing, but seeing that they are going I must say I am really glad because I know it will give pleasure to an 'old soldier' at home, who ought long ago to have had all the medals and distinctions ever conferred.

Early August 1917 was an intensely busy time for Fr Doyle. He had at this stage been appointed chaplain to the Royal Dublin Fusiliers, and had worked closely with Fr Frank Browne SJ, who achieved posthumous fame for his photographic skills[7]. On 3 August, Father

---

7. 1880-1960. Fr Browne's photographic work provides a fascinating insight into life in the early twentieth century. He was a passenger on the Titanic from Belfast to Cobh, and a

Browne was transferred to the Irish Guards, and from this time onwards Fr Doyle served his men as chaplain alone and without rest due to the failure of Fr Browne's replacement to report for duty. The 16th Irish Division (of which the Dublin Fusiliers were part) fought at the front line without relief for days, the victims of gas attacks and constant shelling. The exhausted soldiers suffered tremendous losses.

The precise details surrounding Fr Doyle's death are unclear. But at some time in the late afternoon of 16 August 1917, a group of soldiers lead by 2nd Lieutenants Marlow and Green got into trouble beyond the front line, and Fr Doyle ran to assist them. It seems that Fr Doyle and the two officers were about to take shelter when they were hit by a German shell and killed. His body was never recovered.

Father Doyle's death was a stunning loss to his men. A month after his death, fellow Jesuit chaplain Fr John Delany met some of the 16th Division. In a letter to the Jesuit Provincial in Ireland he wrote that the soldiers:

---

wealthy couple he met on board offered to pay for him to travel to New York, but he disembarked at Cobh under the orders of the Jesuit Provincial, in the process possibly saving his life from the forthcoming disaster. He was the most decorated Catholic chaplain of World War I. Writing about Fr Doyle, Fr Browne exclaimed: 'Fr Doyle is a marvel. You may talk of heroes and saints, they are hardly in it! … We cannot get him away from the line when the men are there … The men couldn't stick it half so well if he weren't there … he wears no tin hat and he is always so cheery'.

were full of Fr Doyle and his exploits. How grieved they are at their sad loss nobody can tell unless they speak to them personally. He seemed to have gripped them all, individually as well as collectively.

Tributes to Fr Doyle poured in, some of which can be read in the appendix on p. 185. But perhaps the most touching testimony to Fr Doyle's popularity among the soldiers was an entirely anonymous and unintended one. One night in January 1922, the then eighty-nine-year-old Hugh Doyle awoke to find a burglar in his house. The thief forced him to open various drawers in the house. Upon coming across a picture of Fr Doyle, the burglar held it up and asked Hugh what his connection was to Fr Doyle. Upon hearing that he was his father, the thief exclaimed, 'that was a holy priest … he saved many souls'. Kissing the picture, he put it in his pocket and left the house empty-handed!

Father Doyle's energetic apostolate as a priest in Ireland, culminating in his cheerful embrace of hardship and death in order to serve his 'poor brave boys' in the trenches, marks him out as an effective, well-loved and zealous priest.

But the story does not end there, for there was much more to Fr Willie Doyle than most people suspected. In his room back in Dublin were his personal papers, with a note asking that they be destroyed if he died. Thankfully, his superiors did not consent to this destruction, and the papers were given to his friend, Professor Alfred O'Rahilly, who was at that time writing a biography of Fr Doyle.

When O'Rahilly's biography, including extensive extracts from Fr Doyle's private notes and diaries, was first published in 1920 it was something of a sensation. The book went through several editions and was translated into all major European languages. The Jesuit Superior General Fr Ledochowsky warmly praised it and had it read in the refectory of the General Curia in Rome, while the famous Jesuit historian and biographer Fr James Brodrick described it as 'one of the finest, wisest, most inspiring and learned religious books ever published'.

Father Doyle's diaries reveal the intensity of his prayer, his personal austerity (often offered up to make reparation for the sins of priests) and his dogged pursuit of holiness. They show him to be a spiritual tactician of the highest order forever focussed on the primary duties of his state in life. As he noted on one occasion: 'To do something great and heroic may never come, but I can make my life heroic by faithfully and daily putting my best effort into each duty as it comes round'. His heroism on the field of battle was the fruit of that earlier daily pursuit of holiness in little things. Some extracts from these diaries can be read in chapter two and a variety of prayers, meditations and snippets of spiritual advice can be read in chapters three through to six.

The combination of Fr Doyle's extraordinary heroism in World War I, the dedicated struggle for holiness revealed in his private notes, and his naturally appealing personality have attracted people from all around the world to him in the century since his death. Within a dozen years of his death the Jesuits had received more than six thousand reports of alleged favours through his intercession. These letters show how truly global the devotion to Fr Doyle was – more than fifty reported favours from India; more than seventy from Africa; more than one hundred from Australia; almost two thousand from the United States ...

Father Doyle's ability to reach out to people from very diverse backgrounds and cultures is a very curious part of his charism. He came from a privileged background and yet he had a rapport with the poor and with ordinary workers; he had the rank of Captain in the army and yet he slummed it with the ordinary soldiers, who were in tears after his death; he was an ardent Catholic yet he was loved by the non-Catholic soldiers and was able to build bridges with those who, for whatever reason, were alienated from the Church.

The same ability to reach out to others seems to have remained in evidence after his death, given the diverse range of people who have been attracted by his life and spirit.

Among Fr Doyle's devotees we can list several canonised saints, including St Alberto Hurtado, a Jesuit from Chile; the Spanish priest St Josemaria Escriva, founder of Opus Dei; and St Teresa of

Calcutta. The Nobel Prize-winning writer and Catholic convert Sigrid Undset was also fascinated with him and intended to write a biography, but sadly she did not manage to do so. But it wasn't just those renowned for their holiness that were attracted to him. Brendan Behan referred to Fr Doyle with praise in his autobiographical *Borstal Boy*, and O'Rahilly's biography of Fr Doyle was apparently among his favourite books.

There were once moves to open Fr Doyle's cause for beatification, but these faded somewhat in the middle part of the last century. But there is now renewed interest in the life and spirit of Fr Doyle as a new generation discovers him on the internet and as the passage of time has given a different perspective on his involvement in the First World War.

The priesthood has lost some of the esteem in which it was once held in Ireland. That is precisely why Fr Doyle's witness is needed now more than ever, and why the time may have come to consider his cause for beatification once again. The Gospel tells us that there is no greater love than to lay down one's life for others. This is exactly what Fr Doyle did, and not only on 16 August 1917, but in his daily struggle to be generous with God and with others. Fr Doyle shows us by the generosity of his life, and especially by the sacrifice of his death, how we should behave as Christians.

Chapter One:
Letters from the Front

This selection of letters and notes focuses mainly on the period from late 1915 until 14 August 1917, three days before Fr Doyle's death. The material is presented chronologically, and most of this chapter originated as correspondence to Mr Hugh Doyle, other members of the family or intimate friends.

On volunteering as a military chaplain, 9 November 1914

I have volunteered for the front as military chaplain, though perhaps I may never be sent. Naturally I have little attraction for the hardship and suffering the life would mean; but it is a glorious chance of making the 'ould body' bear something for Christ's dear sake. However, what decided me in the end was a thought that flashed into my mind when in the chapel: the thought that if I get killed I shall die a martyr of charity and so the longing of my heart will be gratified. This much my offering myself as chaplain has done for me: it has made me realise that my life may be very short and that I must do all I can for Jesus now.

On being accepted as chaplain and departing for war, late November 1915

A last farewell for I shall be far away when you receive this. My *via crucis*[8] is nearly over; but only in heaven will you know how I have suffered all this week. It is all for him and I do not regret it; but he filled my cup of bitterness this evening when I left my darling old father. Thank God, at last I can say, I have given him all; or rather he has taken all from me. May his sweet will be done.

Arrival at Bordon military camp, 1 January 1916

We had an awful time of storm and rain coming over here, but the first thing I saw on reaching the barrack square was a hut marked R.C. Church. I took it for granted that it was just the usual hut set apart for Sunday Mass, but on trying the door you can imagine my delight to find a small but beautifully furnished chapel with a lamp burning before the altar, which made my heart leap with joy.

I felt as if all the hardships of my life had vanished, for I had found him again who makes the hard things easy and the bitter things sweet. What did anything matter now since I could go and tell him all about it and get help and consolation from Jesus. I really think that this month's privation of the Blessed Sacrament has taught me the true value of the tabernacle. But his

---

8. Way of the Cross; path of suffering.

goodness did not stop here; the other priest who had the key gave it to me without my even suggesting it, so I can go to him at any hour of the day or night if I want to. Is he not good to have put the little chapel where he did, as it might have been in any other part of the camp, miles away? I do not think there is a happier man in England than I today. I am writing this, sitting on a piece of wood – no chairs in our quarters. There are about one thousand two hundred Catholics in our brigade now. I get a few 'big fish' each evening.

Before departing for France, 14 February 1916

We are having desperate work these days. The good God is simply pouring out his grace on these poor fellows and reconciling them before they die. It has to be quick work, no time for 'trimmings'. I have positively a pain in my arm giving Absolution and Communions in the morning. I was able to manage exposition all day last Sunday, which brought in many an erring sheep. I realise that from this [time] on my life will be a martyrdom in a way I never thought of. I have got to love my brave lads almost like my own brothers and sisters. They are so wild and reckless, and at the same time so full of faith and love of God and his blessed mother. Yet soon I shall have to see the majority of them blown to bits, torn and mangled out of shape. Our brigade is leaving tomorrow for France. I am waiting till Friday night, so as to get in all the confessions I can. Do pray I may be able to say daily Mass. I shall carry everything necessary on my back, and so may manage the Holy Sacrifice in the train. Whilst here I have given Jesus two things which he often asked, but which I refused through 'prudence and a fear of interfering with important work' – a very old trick of the devil, which my eyes are open to see now. The first was sometimes to fast strictly all day – once I did a hard day's work ending up with a fifteen miles' march on a cup of tea. The second was to spend the whole night in prayer. Including confessions I was able one night to pass eleven hours with Jesus – telling him every five minutes I was going after five more.

First night in the trenches, 31 March 1916

I had rather an amusing experience the first night I spent in the trenches. On arriving here, I found two officers in the dug-out, which was intended for me, but as they were leaving the next day, I did not care to evict them. After some search, I came across an unoccupied, glorified rabbit hole (any port in a storm). It was not too inviting looking, and rather damp, but I got a trench-board which made a capital foundation for a bed and spread my sleeping bag over it. Let me say here that I do not recommend 'trench-boards' for beds. It is simply a kind of ladder with flat steps, which is laid at the bottom of the trench, but being rather narrow requires great skill to prevent yourself from rolling off during the night. In addition, the sharp edges of the steps have a trick of cutting into your back and ribs making you feel in the morning as if you had been at Donnybrook Fair the night before.

In spite of it all I slept soundly till I was awakened by feeling a huge rat sitting on my sheet. The rats round here beat anything I have ever seen. If I told you they were as big as sheep you would scarcely believe me, so let me say a lamb: in any case this fellow was a whopper, weighing fully seven pounds as I proved afterwards ... but as I was gradually awoke more fully I felt his weight and could dimly see the black outline. Before I quite realised what was happening, a warm soft tongue began to lick my face, and I recognised my old friend – the dog!

Burying the dead, 1 April 1916

Taking a short-cut across to our lines I found myself in the first battlefield of Loos, the place where the French had made their attack. For some reason or other this part of the ground had not been cleared, and it remains more or less as it was on the morning of the fight. I had to pick my steps for numbers of unexploded shells, bombs and grenades lay all around. The ground was littered with broken rifles, torn uniform, packs, etc., just as the men had flung them aside, charging the German trenches. Almost the first thing I saw was a human head torn from the trunk, though there was no sign of the body. The soldiers had been buried on the spot as they fell; that is, if you can call [it] burial, hastily throwing a few shovelfuls of clay on the corpses: there was little time, I fancy, for digging graves, and in war time there is not much thought or sentiment for the slain. As I walked along I wondered had they made certain each man was really dead. One poor fellow had been buried, surely, before breath had left his body, for there was every sign of a last struggle and one arm was thrust out from its shroud of clay. A large mound caught my eye. Four pairs of feet were sticking out, one a German, judging by his boots, and three Frenchmen – friend and foe are sleeping their long last sleep in peace together. They were decently covered compared with the next I saw; a handful of earth covered the wasted body, but the legs and arms and head were exposed to view. He seemed quite a young lad with fair, almost golden, hair. 'An unknown soldier' was all the rough wooden cross over him told me about him; but I thought of the sorrowing mother, far away, thinking of her boy who was 'missing', and hoping against hope that he might one day come back. Thank God, heaven one day will reunite them both. I found a shovel near at hand and after a couple of hours' stiff work was able to cover the bodies decently, so that on earth at least they may rest in peace …

Father Doyle's first full war burial later that day

As soon as it was dark we carried the poor fellow out on a stretcher, just as he had fallen, and as quietly as we could, began to dig the grave. It was weird. We were standing in front of the German trenches on two sides, though a fair distance away, and every now and then a star-shell went up, which we felt certain would reveal our presence to the enemy. I put my ritual in the bottom of my hat, and with the aid of an electric torch read the burial service, while the men screened the light with their caps, for a single flash would have turned the machine guns on us. I cannot say if we were seen or not, but all the time bullets came whizzing by, though more than likely stray ones and not aimed at us. Once I had to get the men to lay down, as things were rather warm, but somehow I felt quite safe, as if the dead soldier's guardian angel was sheltering us from all danger, till the poor dust was laid to rest. It was my first war burial, though assuredly not my last – may God rest his soul and comfort those left to mourn him.

Friendly fleas, 22 April 1916

When introducing you to my friends the rats, I made a serious omission in forgetting another class of most attentive friends, smaller in size but more active, in a personal way: they are not called 'Teas' but something very like that. You must remember that the unwashable Hun lived in our cellar for months, and 'departing left behind him' a large number of small fierce warriors from across the Rhine. Next came the French. There is not much picking on a Frenchman, so it is small wonder that when they in turn departed their small companions remained in hope of better things to come. Tommy Atkins then appeared, and not to be outdone left a legacy also. Fortunately, these visitors were natives of different countries, speaking different tongues, otherwise, had they been friends and united in policy, we should have been literally pulled out of bed. These are some of the pleasures of a military campaign and prevent one from ever feeling lonely.

The Hulluch gas attack, 27 April 1916

About four o'clock[9] the thought struck me that it would be a good thing to walk back to the village to warm myself and say an early Mass for the nuns, who usually have to wait hours for some chaplain to turn up. They have been very kind to me, and I was glad of this chance of doing this little service to them. The village is about two miles behind our trench, in such a position that one can leave cover with perfect safety and walk there across the fields. As I left the trench about 4.45, the sun was just rising. It was a perfect morning with a gentle breeze blowing. Now and again came the crack of a rifle, but all was unusually calm and still; little did I think of the deadly storm about to burst and hurry so many brave men into eternity. I had just reached a point half way between our trenches and the village when I heard behind me

---

9.   This refers to 4 a.m.

the deep boom of a German gun quickly followed by a dozen others. In a moment our gunners replied and before I could well realise what was taking place, the air was alive with shells. At first I thought it was just a bit of the usual 'good morning greeting' and that after ten minutes' artillery strafe all would be quiet once more. But I soon saw this was a serious business, for gun after gun, and battery after battery, was rapidly coming into action, until at the lowest number five hundred guns were roaring all round me. It was a magnificent if terrifying sight. The ground fairly shook with the roar of the guns, for the 'heavies' now had taken up the challenge, and all round the horizon I could see the clouds of smoke and dust from the bursting shells as both sides kept searching for their opponents' hidden cannon.

There I stood in the very centre of the battle, the one man of all the thousands engaged who was absolutely safe, for I was away from the trenches, there were no guns or troops near me to draw fire, and though tens of thousands of shells went over my head, not even a splinter fell near me. I felt that the good God had quietly 'dumped' me there till all danger had passed.

After a while seeing that this heavy shelling meant an attack of some kind, and that soon many a dying man would need my help, I turned round and made my way towards the ambulance station. As I approached the trenches I noticed the smoke from the bursting shells, which was hanging thickly over them and was being driven towards me across the fields. For once, I said to myself, I am going to smell the smoke of a real battle, and I stepped out quite gaily—the next moment I had turned and was running back for my life – the Germans had started a poison gas attack which I had mistaken for shell smoke, and I had walked straight into it!

After about twenty yards I stopped to see what was to be done, for I knew it was useless to try and escape by running. I saw (assuredly again providentially) that I had struck the extreme edge of the gas and also that the wind was blowing it away to my left. A hundred yards in the opposite direction, and I was safe.

I must confess for a moment I got a shock, as a gas attack was the very last thing I was thinking about – in fact we thought the Germans had given it up. Fortunately too I had not forgotten the old days of the chemistry room at Ratcliffe College nor Brother Thompson and his 'stink bottles' so I knew at the first whiff it was chlorine gas and time for this child to make tracks.

But I was not yet out of the woods. Even as I was congratulating myself on my good fortune, I saw both right and left of where I stood the green wave of a second gas attack rolling towards me like some huge spectre stretching out its ghostly arms. As I saw it coming, my heart went out to God in one fervent act of gratitude for his goodness to me. As probably you know we all carry 'smoke helmets' slung over our shoulders in a case, to be used against a gas attack. That morning as I was leaving my dugout I threw my helmet aside. I had a fairly long walk before me, the helmet is a bit heavy on a hot day, and as I said, German gas was most unlikely. So I made up my mind to leave it behind. In view of what happened, it may appear imagination now, but a voice seemed to whisper loudly in my ear: 'Take your helmet with you; don't leave without it'. I turned back and slung it over my shoulder. Surely it was the warning voice of my guardian angel, for if I had not done so, you would never have had this letter[10].

I wonder can you picture my feelings at this moment? Here was death in its most awful form sweeping down towards me; thank God I had the one thing which could save me, but with a carelessness for which I ought to be scourged, I had never tried the helmet on and did not know if it were in working order. In theory, with the helmet on I was absolutely safe, but it was an anxious moment waiting for the scorching test, and to make things more horrible, I was absolutely alone. But I had the companionship of one who sustained me in the hour of trial, and kneeling down I took the pyx from my pocket and

---

10. On a subsequent occasion Fr Doyle wrote that 'Some invisible, almost physical, force turned me back to get my helmet'.

received the Blessed Eucharist as viaticum[11]. I had not a moment to spare, and had my helmet just fixed when I was buried in a thick green fog of poison gas. In a few moments my confidence returned for the helmet worked perfectly and I found I was able to breathe without any ill effects from the gas.

By the time I got down to the dressing station the guns had ceased fire, the gas blown away, and the sun was shining in a cloudless sky. Already a stream of wounded was coming in and I soon had my hands full when an urgent message reached me from the front trench. A poor fellow had been desperately wounded, a bullet had cut him like a knife across the stomach, with results you can best imagine. He was told he had only a few minutes to live, and asked if they could do anything for him. 'I have only one wish before I die,' he answered, 'could you possibly get me Fr Doyle? I'll go happy then.' It was hard work to reach him, as parts of the communication trench were knee deep in water and thick mud. Then I was misdirected and sent in the wrong direction, but I kept on praying I might be in time, and at last found the dying man still breathing and conscious. The look of joy, which lit up his face when I knelt beside him, was reward enough for the effort I had made. I gave him absolution and anointed him before he died, but occupied as I was I did not notice that a third gas attack had begun. Before

11. The Eucharist as given to a person near or in danger of death.

I could get my helmet out and on, I had swallowed a couple of mouthfuls, which did me no serious harm beyond making me feel rather sick and weak.

As I made my way slowly up the trench, feeling altogether a poor thing, I stumbled across a young officer who had been badly gassed. He had got his helmet on, but was coughing and choking in a terrible way. 'For God's sake,' he cried, 'help me to tear off this helmet – I can't breathe. I'm dying.' I saw if I left him the end would not be far; so catching hold of him, I half carried, half dragged him up the trench to the medical aid post. I shall never forget that ten minutes, it seemed hours. I seemed to have lost all my strength: struggling with him to prevent him killing himself by tearing off his helmet made me almost forget how to breathe through mine. I was almost stifled, though safe from gas, while the perspiration simply poured from my forehead. I could do nothing but pray for help and set my teeth, for if I once let go, he was a dead man. Thank God, we both at last got to the aid post, and I had the happiness of seeing him in the evening out of danger, though naturally still weak.

Fortunately, this last attack was short and light, so that I was able to take off my helmet and after a cup of tea was all right. The best proof I can give you of this lies in the fact that I have since put in three of the hardest days' work of my life which I could not possibly have done had I been really gassed, as its first effect is to leave one as helpless as a child.

On paper every man with a helmet was as safe as
I was from gas poisoning. But now it is evident many
of the men despised the old German gas, some did not
bother putting on their helmets, others had torn theirs,
and others like myself had thrown them aside or lost
them. From early morning till late at night I worked
my way from trench to trench single handed the first
day, with three regiments to look after, and could get
no help. Many men died before I could reach them;
others seemed just to live till I anointed them, and
were gone before I passed back. There they lay, scores
of them (we lost eight hundred, nearly all from gas) in
the bottom of the trench, in every conceivable posture
of human agony: the clothes torn off their bodies in
a vain effort to breathe; while from end to end of that
valley of death came one low unceasing moan from
the lips of brave men fighting and struggling for life.

I don't think you will blame me when I tell you
that more than once the words of absolution stuck in
my throat, and the tears splashed down on the patient
suffering faces of my poor boys as I leant down to
anoint them. One young soldier seized my two hands
and covered them with kisses; another looked up and
said: 'Oh! Father I can die happy now, sure I'm not
afraid of death or anything else since I have seen you.'
Don't you think, dear father, that the little sacrifice
made in coming out here has already been more than
repaid, and if you have suffered a little anxiety on my
account, you have at least the consolation of knowing

that I have, through God's goodness, been able to comfort many a poor fellow and perhaps to open the gates of heaven for them.

One year later Fr Doyle reflected back on this event and revealed that he hadn't disclosed all of the dangers that he faced during the gas attack.

I have never told you the whole story of that memorable April morning or the repetition of it the following day, or how when I was lying on the stretcher going to 'peg out', as the doctor believed, God gave me back my strength and energy in a way which was nothing short of a miracle, to help many a poor fellow to die in peace and perhaps to open the gates of heaven to not a few.

I had come through the three attacks without ill results, though having been unexpectedly caught by the last one, as I was anointing a dying man and did not see the poisonous fumes coming, I had swallowed some of the gas before I could get my helmet on. It was nothing very serious, but left me rather weak and washy. There was little time to think of that, for wounded and dying were lying all along the trenches, and I was the only priest on that section at the time.

The fumes had quite blown away, but a good deal of the gas, being of a heavy nature, had sunk down to the bottom of the trench and gathered under the duck-boards or wooden flooring. It was impossible to do one's work with the gas helmet on, and so as I knelt down to absolve or anoint man after man for the greater part of that day, I had to inhale the chlorine fumes till I had nearly enough gas in my poor insides to inflate a German sausage balloon.

I did not then know that when a man is gassed his only chance (and a poor one at that) is to lie perfectly still to give the heart a chance of fighting its foe. In happy ignorance of my real state, I covered mile after mile of those trenches until at last in the evening, when the work was done, I was able to rejoin my battalion in a village close to the Line.

It was only then I began to realise that I felt 'rotten bad' as schoolboys say. I remember the doctor, who was a great friend of mine, feeling my pulse and shaking his head as he put me lying in a corner of the shattered house, and then he sat beside me for hours with a kindness I can never forget. He told me afterwards he was sure I was a 'gone coon', but at the moment I did not care much. Then I fell asleep only to be rudely awakened at four next morning by the crash of guns and the dreaded bugle call 'gas alarm, gas alarm'. The Germans had launched a second attack, fiercer than the first. It did not take long to make up my mind what to do – who would hesitate at such a moment, when the reaper Death was busy? – and before I reached the trenches I had anointed a number of poor fellows who had struggled back after being gassed and had fallen dying by the roadside.

The harvest that day was a big one, for there had been bloody fighting all along the Front. Many a man died happy in the thought that the priest's hand had been raised in absolution over his head and the holy oils' anointing had given pardon to those senses which he had used to offend the almighty. It was a long, hard day, a day of heart rending sights, with the consolation of good work done in spite of the deadly fumes, and I reached my billet wet and muddy, pretty nearly worn out, but perfectly well, with not the slightest ill effect from what I had gone through, nor have I felt any since. Surely God has been good to me. That was not the first of his many favours, nor has it been the last.

A narrow escape, June 1916

I was standing in a trench, quite a long distance from the firing line, a spot almost as safe as Dalkey itself, talking to some of my men, when we heard in the distance the scream of a shell. It was evidently one of those random shots which Brother Fritz sends along from time to time, as no other came after it. We very soon became painfully aware that our visitor was heading for us and that if he did not explode in front of our trench his career would certainly come to an end close behind us. I did not feel uneasy for I knew we were practically safe from flying fragments which would pass over our head, but none of us had calculated that this gentleman had made up his mind to drop into the trench itself, a couple of paces from where I stood.

What really took place in the next ten seconds I cannot say: I was conscious of a terrible explosion and the thud of falling stones and debris. I thought the drums of my ears were split by the crash and I believe I was knocked down by the concussion, but when I jumped to my feet I found the two men, who were standing at my left hand, the side the shell fell, stretched on the ground dead, though I think I had time to give them absolution and the last sacraments. The poor fellow on my right was lying badly wounded in the head, but though a bit stunned and dazed by the suddenness of the whole thing, I was absolutely untouched though covered with dirt and blood.

My escape was nothing short of a miracle, for a moment before I was standing on the very spot where the shell fell, and had just moved away a couple of paces. I did not think it was possible for one to be so near a high explosive and not be killed, and even now I cannot account for my marvellous escape. In saying this I am not quite truthful, for I have not a doubt where the saving protection came from. I had made up my mind to consecrate some small hosts at my Mass the following morning, and put them in my pyx as usual, but as I walked through the little village on my way to the trenches the thought came to me that with so much danger about it would be well to have Our Blessed Lord's company and protection. I went into the church, opened the tabernacle, and with the sacred host resting on my heart set out confidently to face whatever lay before me: little did I think I was about to be so near death, or how much depended on that simple action.

The presence of the chaplain, July 1916

As I came along the trench I could hear the men whisper, 'Here's the priest,' while the faces which a moment before had been marked with the awful strain of the waiting lit up with pleasure. As I gave the absolution and the blessing of God on their work, I could not help thinking how many a poor fellow would soon be stretched lifeless a few paces from where he stood; and though I ought to be hardened by this time, I found it difficult to choke down the sadness which filled my heart. 'God bless you, Father, we're ready now,' was reward enough for facing the danger, since every man realised that each moment was full of dreadful possibilities.

The protection of Our Lady's mantle, 15 August 1916

August 15 has always been a day of many graces for me. It is the anniversary of my consecration to Mary and of my vows in the Society ... Knowing there were a good number of my boys about I hurried back as quickly as I could, and made my way up the long, narrow street. The shells were all coming in one direction, across the road, not down it, so that by keeping close to the houses on the shady side there was little danger, though occasional thrills of excitement enough to satisfy Don Quixote himself. I reached the village crossroads in time to lift up the poor sentry who had been badly hit, and with the help of a couple of men carried him to the side of the road. He was unconscious, but I gave him absolution and was half way through the anointing when with a scream and a roar which made our hearts jump a shell whizzed over our heads and crashed into the wall directly opposite on the other side of the street, covering us with brick dust and dirt. Bits of shrapnel came thud, thud, on the ground and wall around us, but neither I nor the men were touched.

'Begorra, Father, that was a near one, anyhow,' said one of them, as he brushed the dust off his tunic, and started to fill his pipe. 'It was well we had your Reverence with us when Jerry[12] sent that one across.'

'You must not thank me, boys,' I said, 'don't you know it is our Lady's feast, and Mary had her mantle spread over us to save us from all harm?'

'True for you, Father,' came the answer. But I could see by their faces that they were by no means convinced that I had not worked the miracle.

Though it was 15 August I was taking no risks, especially with this reputation to maintain! So, the poor boy being dead, I bundled the rest of them down a cellar out of harm's way, and started off again …

---

12. A nickname for a German.

One man was beyond my aid, a few slightly wounded, and that was all. As I came round the corner of the church I met four of my boys calmly strolling along in the middle of the street as if they were walking on Kingstown pier. I won't record what I said, but my words helped by the opportune arrival of an unpleasantly near H.E.[13] had the desired effect, and we all took cover in the church. It was only then I realised my mistake, for it soon became evident the Germans were firing at the church itself. One after another the shells came in rapid succession, first on one side then on the other, dropping in front and behind the building, which was a target with its tall, white tower. It was madness to go out, and I do not think the men, some score of them, knew of their danger, nor did I tell them, but 'man of little faith,' as I was, I cast anxious eyes at the roof and wished it were stronger. All's well that ends well, they say. Not a shot hit the church, though the houses and road got it hot. Our fiery ordeal ended at last, safely and happily for all of us. And 15 August 1916 went down on my list as another day of special grace and favour at Mary's hands.

The horror of the Battle of the Somme, September 1916

I have been through the most terrible experience of my whole life, in comparison with which all that I

---

13. High explosive.

have witnessed or suffered since my arrival in France seems of little consequence; a time of such awful horror that I believe if the good God had not helped me powerfully by his grace I could never have endured it. To sum up all in one word, for the past week I have been living literally in hell, amid sights and scenes and dangers enough to test the courage of the bravest; but through it all my confidence and trust in our Blessed Lord's protection never wavered, for I felt that somehow, even if it needed a miracle, he would bring me safe through the furnace of tribulation. I was hit three times, on the last occasion by a piece of shell big enough to have taken off half my leg, but wonderful to relate I did not receive a wound or scratch – there is some advantage, you see, in having a good thick skin! As you can imagine, I am pretty well worn out and exhausted, rather shaken by the terrific strain of those days and nights without any real sleep or repose, with nerves tingling, ever on the jump, like the rest of us; but it is all over now; we are well behind the firing line on our way at last for a good long rest, which report says will be enjoyed close to the sea.

That evening just as we were sitting down for dinner, spread on a pile of empty shell boxes, urgent orders reached us to march in ten minutes. There was only time to grab a slice of bread, and hack off a piece of meat before rushing to get one's kit. As luck would have it, I had had nothing to eat since the morning, and was famished, but there was nothing for it but to tighten one's belt and look happy. After a couple of hours' tramp a halt was called. 'All impediments, kits, packs, blankets to be stacked by the side of the road,' came the order. This meant business evidently as we set off again with nothing but our arms and the clothes we stood in. If it rained we got wet, and when it got dry we got dry too, jolly prospect, but 'c'est la guerre,' war is war. I held on to my Mass things, but to my great sorrow, for five days I was not able to offer the holy sacrifice, the biggest privation of the whole campaign. One good result at least came from this trial: it showed me in a way I never realised before, what a help daily Mass is in one's life…

I was standing about one hundred yards away watching a party of my men crossing the valley, when I saw the earth under their feet open and the twenty men disappear in a cloud of smoke, while a column of stones and clay was shot a couple of hundred feet into the air. A big German shell by the merest chance had landed in the middle of the party. I rushed down the slope, getting a most unmerciful 'whack' between the shoulders, probably from a falling stone, as it did not wound me, but it was no time to think of one's safety. I gave them all a general absolution, scraped the clay from the faces of a couple of buried men who were not wounded, and then anointed as many of the poor lads as I could reach. Two of them had no faces to anoint and others were ten feet under the clay, but a few were living still. By this time half a dozen volunteers had run up and were digging the buried men out. War may be horrible, but it certainly brings out the best side of a man's character; over and over again I have seen men risking their lives to help or save a comrade, and these brave fellows knew the risk they were taking, for when a German shell falls in a certain place, you clear as quickly as you can since several more are pretty certain to land close. It was a case of duty for me, but real courage for them. We dug like demons for our lads' lives and our own, to tell the truth, for every few minutes another 'iron pill' from a Krupp gun would come tearing down the valley, making our very hearts leap into our mouths. More than once we were well sprinkled with clay and stones, but the cup of cold water promise was well kept, and not one of the party received a scratch. We got three buried men out alive, not much the worse for their trying experience, but so thoroughly had the shell done its work that there was not a single wounded man in the rest of the party; all had gone to a better land. As I walked back I nearly shared the fate of my boys, but somehow escaped again, and pulled out two more lads who were only buried up to the waist and uninjured. Meanwhile the regiment had been ordered back to a safer position on the hill, and we were able to breathe once more…

To make matters worse we were posted fifteen yards in front of two batteries of field guns, while on our right a little further off were half a dozen huge sixty-pounders; not once during the whole night did these guns cease firing … I could not help thinking of him who often had nowhere to lay his head, and it helped me to resemble him a little …

The first part of our journey lay through a narrow trench, the floor of which consisted of deep thick mud, and the bodies of dead men trodden under foot. It was horrible beyond description, but there was no help for it, and on the half-rotten corpses of our own brave men we marched in silence, everyone busy with his own thoughts. I shall spare you gruesome details, but you can picture one's sensations as one felt the ground yield under one's foot, and one sank down through the body of some poor fellow.

Half an hour of this brought us out on the open into the middle of the battlefield of some days previous. The wounded, at least I hope so, had all been removed, but the dead lay there stiff and stark, with open staring eyes, just as they had fallen. Good God, such a sight! I had tried to prepare myself for this, but all I had read or pictured gave me little idea of the reality. Some lay as if they were sleeping quietly, others had died in agony, or had had the life crushed out of them by mortal fear, while the whole ground, every foot of it, was littered with heads or limbs or pieces of torn human bodies. In the bottom of one hole lay a British and a German soldier, locked in a deadly embrace, neither had any weapon, but they had fought on to the bitter end. Another couple seemed to have realised that the horrible struggle was none of their making, and that they were both children of the same God; they had died hand-in-hand praying for and forgiving one another. A third face caught my eye, a tall, strikingly handsome young German, not more, I should say, than eighteen. He lay there calm and peaceful, with a smile of happiness on his face, as if he had had a glimpse of heaven before he died. Ah, if only his poor mother could have seen her boy it would have soothed the pain of her broken heart.

We pushed on rapidly through that charnel house, for the stench was fearful, till we stumbled across a sunken road. Here the retreating Germans had evidently made a last desperate stand, but had been caught by our artillery fire. The dead lay in piles, the blue grey uniforms broken by many a khaki-clad body. I saw the ruins of what was evidently the dressing station, judging by the number of bandaged men about; but a shell had found them out even here and swept them all into the net of death.

A halt for a few minutes gave me the opportunity I was waiting for. I hurried along from group to group, and as I did the men fell on their knees to receive absolution. A few words to give them courage, for no man knew if he would return alive. A 'God bless and protect you, boys,' and I passed on to the next company. As I did, a soldier stepped out of the ranks, caught me by the hand, and said: 'I am not a Catholic, sir, but I want to thank you for that beautiful prayer.'

The regiments moved on to the wood, while the doctor and I took up our positions in the dressing station to wait for the wounded. This was a dug-out on the hill facing Leuze Wood, and had been in German occupation the previous afternoon ...

Fighting was going on all round, so that I was kept busy, but all the time my thoughts and my heart were with my poor boys in the wood opposite. They had reached it safely, but the Germans somehow had worked round the sides and temporarily cut them off. No food or water could be sent up, while ten slightly wounded men who tried to come back were shot down, one after another. To make matters worse, our own artillery began to shell them, inflicting heavy losses, and though repeated messages were sent back, continued doing so for a long time. It appears the guns had fired so much that they were becoming worn out, making the shells fall three hundred yards short.

Under these circumstances it would be madness to try and reach the wood, but my heart bled for the wounded and dying lying there alone. When dusk came I made up my mind to try and creep through the valley, more especially as the fire had slackened very much, but once again the Providence of God watched over me. As I was setting out I met a sergeant who argued the point with me ... The poor fellow was so much in earnest I decided to wait a little at least. It was well I did so, for shortly afterwards the Germans opened a terrific bombardment and launched a counter attack on the wood. Some of the Cornwalls, who were holding a corner of the wood, broke and ran, jumping right on top of the Fusiliers. Brave Paddy from the Green Isle stood his ground … and drove the Germans back with cold steel.

Meanwhile we on the opposite hill were having a most unpleasant time. A wounded man had reported that the enemy had captured the wood. Communication was broken and headquarters had no information of what was going on. At that moment an orderly dashed in with the startling news that the Germans were in the valley, and actually climbing our hill. We non-combatants might easily escape to the rear, but who would protect the wounded? They could not be abandoned. If it were daylight the Red Cross would give us protection, but in the darkness of the night the enemy would not think twice about flinging a dozen bombs down the steps of the dug-out. I looked round at the bloodstained walls and shivered. A nice coward, am I not? Thank God, the situation was not quite so bad as reported; our men got the upper hand, and drove back the attack, but that half-hour of suspense will live long in my memory.

Mass for the dead at the Somme, September 1916

By cutting a piece out of the side of the trench, I was just able to stand in front of my tiny altar, a biscuit box supported on two German bayonets. God's angels, no doubt, were hovering overhead, but so were the shells, hundreds of them, and I was a little afraid that when the earth shook with the crash of the guns, the chalice might be overturned. Round about me on every side was the biggest congregation I ever had: behind the altar, on either side, and in front, row after row, sometimes crowding one upon the other, but all quiet and silent, as if they were straining their ears to catch every syllable of that tremendous act of sacrifice – but every man was dead! Some had lain there for a week and were foul and horrible to look at, with faces black and green. Others had only just fallen, and seemed rather sleeping than dead, but there they lay, for none had time to bury them, brave fellows, every one, friend and foe alike, while I held in my unworthy hands the God of Battles, their Creator and their Judge, and prayed him to give rest to their souls. Surely that Mass for the Dead, in the midst of, and surrounded by the dead, was an experience not easily to be forgotten.

The tragic tale of the plum pudding

13 December 1916

As I write, a huge plum pudding[14]… has just walked in the door. A hundred thousand welcomes! The Lord grant I don't get killed till after Christmas at least, it would be a fearful disaster to leave that treasure behind.

---

14. The Christmas pudding was sent as a gift by his sister-in-law.

22 December 1916

A villain of a rat worked his way into the middle of the pudding and built itself a home there. There was not much of the plum pudding left after that but the remainder was all the sweeter.

Reflections on trench life, 19 December 1916

Here I am in a bit of a hole in the side of a ditch, so low that I cannot stand upright and have to bend my head and shoulders during Mass – I can tell you my back aches at the end. My only window is the door (without a door) through which the wind blows day and night; and a cold wind it is just now. I was offered a little stove but … it never came. My home would be fairly dry if I could keep out the damp mists and persuade the drops of water not to trickle from the roof. As a rule I sleep well, though one is often roused to attend some poor fellow who has been hit. Still it is rather reversing the order of things to be glad to get up in the morning to try and get warm; and it is certainly not pleasant to be wakened from sweet dreams by a huge rat burrowing under your pillow or scampering over your face! This has actually happened to me. There is no great luxury in the matter of food, as you may well guess. Recently, owing to someone's carelessness, or possibly because the bag was made to pay toll on the way up to the trenches, my day's rations consisted of half a pot of jam and a piece of cheese!

Through all this, and much in addition, the one thought ever in my mind is the goodness and love of God in choosing me to lead this life, and thus preparing me without a chance of refusal for the work he wants doing. No amount of reading or meditating could have proved to me so convincingly that a life of privation, suffering and sacrifice, accepted lovingly for the love of Jesus, is a life of great joy, and surely of great graces. You see, therefore, that I have reasons in abundance for being happy, and I am truly so.

Hence you ought to be glad that I have been counted worthy to suffer something for our dear Lord, the better to be prepared to do his work. Ask him, won't you, that I may not lose this golden opportunity, but may profit to the full by the graces he is giving me.

Shaking like a leaf, 21 December 1916

It is a curious thing that I have never had a moment's hesitation nor ever felt fear in going into the greatest danger when duty called and some poor chap needed help. But to sit in cold blood, so to speak, and to wait to be blown to pieces or buried by a crump[15] is an experience which tests one's nerves to the limit. Thank God, I have been able to conceal my feelings and so to help others to despise the danger, when I was just longing to take to my heels. An officer said to me at the Somme, 'I have often envied you your coolness and cheerfulness in hot corners'. I rather surprised him by saying that my real feeling was abject fear and I often shook like a leaf ...

---

15. Slang for a German shell.

Three of my lads came tearing in to my dug-out; they had nearly been sent to glory and felt they were safe with the priest. The poor priest cracks a joke or two, makes them forget their terror, and goes on with his lunch while every morsel sticks in his throat from fear and dread of the next shell. A moment passes, one, two, here it comes; dead silence and anxious faces for a second, and then we all laugh, for it is one of our own shells going over. Five minutes more and we know all danger has passed.

Midnight Mass, 24 December 1916

I sang the Mass ... One of the Tommies, from Dolphin's Barn, sang the Adeste beautifully with just a touch of the sweet Dublin accent to remind us of 'home, sweet home,' the whole congregation joining in the chorus. It was a curious contrast: the chapel packed with men and officers, almost strangely quiet and reverent (the nuns were particularly struck by this), praying and singing most devoutly, while the big tears ran down many a rough cheek: outside the cannon boomed and the machine-guns spat out a hail of lead: peace and good will – hatred and bloodshed! It was a midnight Mass none of us will ever forget. A good five hundred men came to Holy Communion, so that I was more than rewarded for my work.

Peace at any price, 1 January 1917

How little the expression 'we were shelled for two hours' conveys to you! People read in their papers some mornings, 'The enemy fiercely attacked our trenches but were driven back again' and never give a thought to the brave fellows who lie in heaps mangled and bleeding, nor to the moans of pain, nor the broken hearts in many a home. Not many at home care much, I fear, otherwise we should hear less of these brave speeches about 'no peace at any price' from men who will never have to fight. If only the world, Allied and German, could see and hear what we see and hear daily there would soon be a shout for 'peace *at any price*'.

Night calls, 13 January 1917

'Two men badly wounded in the firing line, Sir.' I was fast asleep, snugly tucked up in my blankets, dreaming a pleasant dream of something 'hot'. One always dreams of lovely hot things at night in the trenches, sitting at a warm fire at home, or of huge piles of food and drink, but always steaming hot.

'You will need to be quick, Father, to find them alive.' By this time I had grasped the fact that someone was calling me, that some poor dying man needed help, that perhaps a soul was in danger. In a few seconds I had pulled on my big boots, I know I should want them in the mud and wet, jumped into my waterproof and darted down the trench.

It was just two a.m., bitterly cold and snowing hard. God help the poor fellows holding the tumbled in ditch which is called the Front Line, standing there wet and more than frozen, hour after hour; but more than all, God help and strengthen the victims of this war, the wounded soldier with his torn and bleeding body lying out in this awful biting cold, praying for the help that seems so slow in coming.

The first part of my journey was easy enough, except that the snow made it difficult to keep one's feet, and I began to realise that one cannot run as easily at forty-four as one could at twenty-four.

All went well till I reached a certain part of the trench, which rejoices in the attractive name of 'Suicide Corner,' from the fact that the Germans have a machine gun trained on it and at intervals during the night pump a shower of lead on that spot in the hope of knocking out some chance passer-by.

It was just my luck that as I came near this place I heard the 'Rat-tat-tat' of the beastly gun and the whiz of the passing bullets. It was not a pleasant prospect to run the gauntlet and skip through the bullets 'made in Germany' but what priest would hesitate for a second with two dying men at the end of the trench? I ducked my head and 'chivvied' down that trench. (I do not know what this word means, but I believe it implies terrific speed and breathless excitement.) …

Away on my left as I ran I could hear in the stillness of the night the grinding 'Rat-tat-tat' of the machine gun, for all the world as if a hundred German carpenters were driving nails into my coffin, while overhead 'crack, crack, whiz, whiz' went the bullets tearing one after another for fear they would be too late…

The first man was 'in extremis' when I reached him. I did all I could for him, commended his soul to the merciful God as he had only a few minutes to live, and hurried on to find the other wounded boy…

I found the dying lad, he was not much more, so tightly jammed into a corner of the trench it was almost impossible to get him out. Both legs were smashed, one in two or three places, so his chances of life were small as there were other injuries as well. What a harrowing picture that scene would have made. A splendid young soldier, married only a month they told me, lying there pale and motionless in the mud and water with the life crushed out of him by a cruel shell. The stretcher bearers hard at work binding up as well as they may his broken limbs; round about a group of silent Tommies looking on and wondering when will their turn come. Peace for a moment seems to have taken possession of the battlefield; not a sound save the deep boom of some far-off gun and the stifled moans of the dying boy, while as if anxious to hide the scene, nature drops her soft mantle of snow on the living and dead alike. Then while every head is bared come the solemn words of absolution, 'Ego te absolvo,' I absolve thee from thy sins. Depart Christian soul and may the Lord Jesus Christ receive thee with a smiling and benign countenance. Amen.

Oh! surely the gentle Saviour did receive with open arms the brave lad … and as I turned away I felt happy in the thought that his soul was already safe in that land where 'God will wipe away all sorrow from our eyes, for weeping and mourning shall be no more'.

Living with corpses, 17 January 1917

I thought our dug-out in one of the trenches at Loos was bad enough. One end of it had been blown in by a big shell, burying two men, whom it was impossible to get out, and we lived at the other. They, poor chaps, were covered with clay, but not deep enough to keep out the smell of decaying bodies, which did not help one's appetite at meal time, and then when your nerves were more jumpy than usual, you could swear you saw the dead man's boot moving, as if he were still alive.

Coping with cold, January 1917

Before I have finished dressing in the mornings, not a very long process, the water in which I washed is frozen again. One has to be very careful, too, of one's feet, keeping them well rubbed with whale oil, if not you would find yourself unable to walk with half a dozen frozen toes. The dug-out is not the warmest of spots just at present, but even if I felt inclined to growl I would be ashamed to do so seeing what the poor men are suffering in the trenches … I think the limit was reached when the wine froze in the chalice at Mass and a lamp had to be procured to melt it before going on with the consecration. I am thinking it will take fifty lamps to thaw out the poor chaplain.

A good harvest, 19 March 1917

We reap a good harvest with confessions every day at any time the men care to come, but there are many who, for one reason or another, cannot get away before going into the trenches, which nearly always means death for some poor fellows, we give them a general absolution. I do not think there can be a more touching or soul-inspiring sight than to see a whole regiment go down upon their knees to hear that wave of prayer go up to Heaven, as hundreds of voices repeat the Act of Contrition in unison, 'My God, I am heartily sorry that I have ever offended you'. There is an earnestness and a depth of feeling in their voices which tells of real sorrow, even if one did not see the tears gather in the eyes of more than one brave man – and then the deep reverent silence as the priest raises his hand over the bowed heads and pronounces the words of forgiveness. Human nature is ever human nature, and even Irish soldiers commit sins; you can picture then the feelings of the priest standing before that kneeling throng knowing that, by the power of God, his words have washed every soul pure and white at the words of absolution and to watch the look of peace and happiness on the men's faces as they lift their rifles and fall into rank … Don't you agree with me that the consolations and real joys of my life far outweigh the hard things and privations?

Brief respite: cycling trip to Amettes, France, May 1917

I went along leisurely, having plenty of time, for I knew the Sisters would put me up for the night and so made many little detours to visit some of the churches, which are always interesting …

I reached the convent late in the evening, after a most enjoyable and restful ride through the country, away from the din and roar of war. The Sister who opened the door looked at me with all her eyes in a dazed, frightened sort of way. 'I remember you perfectly, Father,' she said, 'but I think I had better let the Mother know first,' and she vanished like a flash, leaving me rather mystified. In a few moments old Mother Hen and all her Chicks came swarming in: 'Mais, mon père, you are dead! We saw in the paper that you were killed by a shell – Fr Doyle, S.J., n'est ce pas?' I then told her about Fr Denis Doyle SJ who, God rest his soul, has got me so many Masses and prayers by mistake. Thereupon all fell on each other's neck and wept. The convent larder was next emptied and, for a dead man, I did remarkably well, ending with a glorious sleep.

The Battle of Messines Ridge, 7 June 1917

It wanted half an hour to zero time – the phrase used for the moment of attack. The guns had ceased firing, to give their crews a breathing space before the storm of battle broke; for a moment at least there was peace on earth and a calm which was almost more trying than the previous roar to us who knew what was coming. A prisoner told us that the enemy knew we were about to attack, but did not expect it for another couple of days. I pictured to myself our men, row upon row waiting in the darkness for the word to charge, and on the other side the Germans in their trenches and dug-outs, little thinking that seven huge mines were laid under their feet, needing only a spark to blow them into eternity. The tension of waiting was terrific, the strain almost unbearable. One felt inclined to scream out and send them warning. But all I could do was to stand on top of the trench and give them absolution, trusting to God's mercy to speed it so far.

Even now I can scarcely think of the scene which followed without trembling with horror. Punctually to the second at 3.10 a.m. there was a deep muffled roar; the ground in front of where I stood rose up, as if some giant had wakened from his sleep and was bursting his way through the earth's crust, and then I saw seven huge columns of smoke and flames shoot hundreds of feet into the air, while masses of clay and stones, tons in weight, were hurled about like pebbles. I never before realised what an earthquake was like, for not only did the ground quiver and shake, but actually rocked backwards and forwards, so that I kept on my feet with difficulty[16]...

---

16. The Battle of Messines Ridge involved almost a million pounds of explosives in a series of mines under the German lines. The explosion was heard as far away as England and was, at that point in time, the largest man-made explosion in history.

Before the debris of the mines had begun to fall to earth, the 'wild Irish' were over the top of the trenches and on the enemy, though it seemed certain they must be killed to a man by the falling avalanche of clay. Even a stolid English colonel standing near was moved to enthusiasm: 'My God!' he said, 'what soldiers! They fear neither man nor devil!' Why should they? They had made their peace with God. He had given them his own sacred body to eat that morning, and they were going out now to face death, as only Irish Catholic lads can do, confident of victory and cheered by the thought that the reward of heaven was theirs ...

Meanwhile hell itself seemed to have been let loose. With the roar of the mines came the deafening crash of our guns, hundreds of them. This much I can say: never before, even in this war, have so many batteries especially of heavy pieces been concentrated on one objective, and how the Germans were able to put up the resistance they did was a marvel to everybody, for our shells fell like hail stones. In a few moments they took up the challenge, and soon things on our side became warm and lively.

In a short time the wounded began to come in, and a number of German prisoners, many of them wounded, also. I must confess my heart goes out to these unfortunate soldiers, whose sufferings have been terrific. I can't share the general sentiment that 'they deserve what they get and one better'. For after all are they not children of the same loving saviour who said:

'Whatever you do to one of these my least ones you do it to me'. I try to show them any little kindness I can, getting them a drink, taking off the boots from smashed and bleeding feet, or helping to dress their wounds, and more than once I have seen the eyes of these rough men fill with tears as I bent over them, or felt my hand squeezed in gratitude.

My men did not go over in the first wave; they were held in reserve to move up as soon as the first objective was taken, hold the position and resist any counter attack. Most of them were waiting behind a thick sand-bag wall not far from the advanced dressing station where I was, which enabled me to keep an eye upon them.

The shells were coming over thick and fast now, and at last, what I expected and feared happened. A big crump hit the wall fair and square, blew three men into the field fifty yards away, and buried five others who were in a small dug-out. For a moment I hesitated, for the horrible sight fairly knocked the 'starch' out of me and a couple more crumps did not help to restore my courage.

I climbed over the trench and ran across the open, as abject a coward as ever walked on two legs, till I reached the three dying men, and then the 'perfect trust' came back to me and I felt no fear. A few seconds sufficed to absolve and anoint my poor boys, and I jumped to my feet, only to go down on my face faster than I got up, as an express train from Berlin roared by.

The five buried men were calling for help, but the others standing around seemed paralysed with fear, all save one sergeant, whose language was worthy of the occasion and rose to a noble height of sublimity. He was working like a Trojan, tearing the sand-bags aside, and welcomed my help with a mingled blessing and curse. The others joined in with pick and shovel, digging and pulling, till the sweat streamed from our faces, and the blood from our hands, but we got three of the buried men out alive, the other two had been killed by the explosion.

Once again I had evidence of the immense confidence our men have in the priest. It was quite evident they were rapidly becoming demoralised, as the best of troops will who have to remain inactive under heavy shell fire. Little groups were running from place to place for greater shelter, and the officers seemed to have lost control. I walked along the line of men, crouching behind the sand-bag wall, and was amused to see the ripple of smiles light up the terrified lads' faces, (so many are mere boys) as I went by. By the time I got back again the men were laughing and chatting as if all danger was miles away, for quite unintentionally, I had given them courage by walking along without my gas mask or steel helmet, both of which I had forgotten in my hurry.

When the regiment moved forward, the doctor and I went with it. By this time the 'impregnable' ridge was in our hands and the enemy retreating down the far side. I spent the rest of that memorable day wandering over the battle field looking for the wounded, and had the happiness of helping many a poor chap, for shells were flying about on all sides.

As I knew there was no chance of saying Mass the next morning, I had taken the precaution of bringing several consecrated particles with me, so that I should not be deprived of Holy Communion. It was the Feast of Corpus Christi and I thought of the many processions of the Blessed Sacrament which were being held at that moment all over the world. Surely there never was a stranger one than mine that day, as I carried the God of Consolation in my unworthy arms over the blood-stained battle field. There was no music to welcome his coming save the scream of a passing shell; the flowers that strewed his path were the broken, bleeding bodies of those for whom he had once died; and the only altar of repose he could find was the heart of one who was working for him alone, striving in a feeble way to make him some return for all his love and goodness.

I shall make no attempt to describe the battlefield. Thank God, our casualties were extraordinarily light, but there was not a yard of ground on which a shell had not pitched, which made getting about very laborious, sliding down one crater and climbing up the next, and also increased the difficulty of finding the wounded.

Providence certainly directed my steps on two occasions at least. I came across one young soldier horribly mutilated, all his intestines hanging out, but quite conscious and able to speak to me. He lived long enough to receive the last sacraments, and died in peace. Later on in the evening I was going in a certain direction when something made me turn back when I saw in the distance a man being carried on a stretcher. He belonged to the artillery, and had no chance of seeing a priest for a long time, but he must have been a good lad, for Mary did not forget him 'at the hour of his death'.

The things I remember best of that day of twenty-four hours' work are: the sweltering heat, a devouring thirst which comes from the excitement of battle, physical weakness from want of food, and a weariness and 'footsoreness' which I trust will pay a little at least of St Peter's heavy score against me.

Three brothers bid farewell, 12 June 1917

There were many little touching incidents during these days, one especially I shall not easily forget. When the men had left the field after the evening devotions I noticed a group of three young boys, brothers I think, still kneeling saying another Rosary. They knew it was probably their last meeting on earth and they seemed to cling to one another for mutual comfort and strength and instinctively turned to the Blessed Mother to help them in their hour of need. There they knelt as if they were alone and unobserved, their hands clasped and faces turned towards heaven, with such a look of beseeching earnestness that the

'Mother of Mercy' must have heard their prayer: 'Holy Mary pray for us now at the hour of our death. Amen.'

Towards the end

30 July 1917

Mass in the open this morning under a drizzling rain was a trying if edifying experience. Colonel, officers and men knelt on the wet grass with the water trickling off them, while a happy if somewhat damp chaplain moved from rank to rank giving every man Holy Communion. Poor fellows: with all their faults God must love them dearly for their simple faith and love of their religion, and for the confident way in which they turn to him for help in the hour of trial.

Many a time one's heart grows sick to think how few will ever see home and country again, for their pluck and daring have marked them down for the positions which only the Celtic dash can take: a post of honour, no doubt, but it means slaughter as well.

We moved off at 10 p.m., a welcome hour in one way, as it means marching in the cool of the night instead of sweating under a blazing sun. Still when one has put in a long day of hard work, and legs and body are pretty well tired out already, the prospect of a stiff march is not too pleasant.

31 July 1917

It was 1.30 a.m. when our first halting place was reached, and as we march again at three, little time was wasted getting to sleep. It was the morning of 31 July, the Feast of St Ignatius, a day dear to every Jesuit, but doubly so to the soldier sons of the soldier saint. Was it to be Mass or sleep? Nature said sleep, but grace won the day, and while the weary soldiers slumbered the adorable sacrifice was offered for them, that God would bless them in the coming fight and, if it were his holy will, bring them safely through it. Mass and thanksgiving over, a few precious moments of rest on the floor of the hut, and we have fallen into line once more.

As we do, the dark clouds are lit up with red and golden flashes of light, the earth quivers with the simultaneous crash of thousands of guns and in imagination we can picture the miles of our trenches spring to life as the living stream of men pours over the top: the Fourth Battle of Ypres has begun.

Men's hearts beat faster, and nerves seem to stretch and vibrate like harp strings as we march steadily on ever nearer and nearer towards the raging fight, on past battery after battery of huge guns and howitzers belching forth shells which ten men could scarcely lift, on past the growing streams of motor ambulances, each with its sad burden of broken bodies, the first drops of that torrent of wounded which will pour along the road. I fancy not a few were wondering how long would it be till they were carried past in the same way, or was this the last march they would ever make till the final roll call on the Great Review Day…

It was nearly eight o'clock, and our dinner was simmering in the pot with a tempting odour, when the fatal telegram came: the battalion will move forward in support at once. I was quite prepared for this little change of plans having experienced such surprises before, and had taken the precaution of laying in a solid lunch early in the day. I did not hear a single growl from anyone, though it meant we had to set out for another march hungry and dinnerless, with the prospect of passing a second night without sleep.

On the road once more in strict fighting kit, the clothes we stood in, a rain coat, and a stout heart. A miserable night with a cold wind driving the drizzling rain into our faces and the ground underfoot being rapidly churned into a quagmire of slush and mud ...

The road was a sight never to be forgotten. On one side marched our column in close formation, on the other galloped by an endless line of ammunition wagons, extra guns hurrying up to the front, and motor lorries packed with stores of all kinds, while between the two flowed back the stream of empties and ambulance after ambulance filled with wounded and dying.

In silence, save for the never ceasing roar of the guns and the rumble of cart wheels, we marched on through the city of the dead, Ypres, not a little anxious, for a shower of shells might come at any minute. Ruin and desolation, desolation and ruin, is the only description I can give of a spot once the pride and glory of Belgium. The hand of war has fallen heavy on the city of Ypres; scarce a stone remains of the glorious cathedral and equally famous Cloth Hall; the churches, a dozen of them, are piles of rubbish, gone are the convents, the hospitals and public buildings, and though many of the inhabitants are still there, their bodies lie buried in the ruins of their homes, and the smell of rotting corpses poisons the air. I have seen strange sights in the last two years, but this was the worst of all. Out again by the opposite gate of this stricken spot ... across the moat and along the road pitted all over with half-filled in shell-holes. Broken carts and dead horses, with human bodies too if one looked, lie on all sides, but one is too weary to think of anything except how many more miles must be covered.

A welcome halt at last with, perhaps, an hour or more delay. The men were already stretched by the side of the road, and I was not slow to follow their example. I often used to wonder how anyone could sleep lying in mud or water, but at that moment the place for sleep, as far as I was concerned, did not matter two straws, a thorn bush, the bed of a stream, anywhere would do to satisfy the longing for even a few moments slumber after nearly two days and nights of marching without sleep. I picked out a soft spot on the ruins of a home, lay down with a sigh of relief, and then, for all I cared, all the king's guns and the kaiser's combined might roar till they were hoarse, and all the rain in the heavens might fall, as it was falling then, I was too tired and happy to bother.

5 August 1917
All day I have been busy hearing the men's confessions, and giving batch after batch Holy Communion. A consolation surely to see them crowding to the sacraments, but a sad one too, because I know for many of them it is the last absolution they will ever receive, and the next time they meet our Blessed Lord will be when they see him face to face in heaven.

My poor brave boys! They are lying now out on the battle-field; some in a little grave dug and blessed by their chaplain, who loves them all as if they were his own children; others stiff and stark with staring eyes, hidden in a shell-hole where they had crept to die; while perhaps in some far-off thatched cabin an anxious mother sits listening for the well-known step and voice which will never gladden her ear again. Do you wonder in spite of the joy that fills my heart that many a time the tears gather in my eyes, as I think of those who are gone?

As the men stand lined up on parade, I go from company to company giving a general absolution which I know is a big comfort to them, and then I shoulder my pack and make for the train which this time is to carry us part of our journey...

Though we are in fighting kit, there is no small load to carry: a haversack containing little necessary things, and three days rations which consist of tinned corn beef, hard biscuits, tea and sugar, with usually some solidified methylated spirit for boiling water when a fire cannot be lighted; two full water-bottles; a couple of gas-helmets the new one weighing nine pounds, but guaranteed to keep out the smell of the Old Boy himself; then a waterproof trench coat; and in addition my Mass kit strapped on my back on the off chance that some days at least I may be able to offer the holy sacrifice on the spot where so many men have fallen. My orderly should carry this, but I prefer to leave him behind when we go into action, to which he does not object. On a roasting hot day, tramping along a dusty road or scrambling up and down shell-holes, the extra weight tells...

As I marched through Ypres at the head of the column, an officer ran across the road and stopped me: 'Are you a Catholic priest?' he asked, 'I should like to go to Confession.' There and then, by the side of the road, while the men marched by, he made his peace with God, and went away, let us hope, as happy as I felt at that moment. It was a trivial incident, but it brought home vividly to me what a priest was and the wondrous power given him by God. All the time we were pushing on steadily towards our goal across the battle-field of the previous week. Five days almost continuous rain had made the torn ground worse than any ploughed field, but none seemed to care as so far not a shot had fallen near.

We were congratulating ourselves on our good luck, when suddenly the storm burst. Away along the front trenches we saw the S.O.S. signal shoot into the air, two red and two green rockets, telling the artillery behind of an attack and calling for support. There was little need to send any signal as the enemy's guns had opened fire with a crash, and in a moment pandemonium, in fact fifty of them were set loose. I can but describe the din by asking you to start together fifty first class thunder storms, though even then the swish and scream, the deafening crash of the shells, would be wanting.

On we hurried in the hope of reaching cover which was close at hand, when right before us the enemy started to put down a heavy barrage, literally a curtain of shells, to prevent reinforcements coming up. There was no getting through that alive and, to make matters worse, the barrage was creeping nearer and nearer, only fifty yards away, while shell fragments hummed uncomfortably close. Old shell-holes there were in abundance, but every one of them was brim full of water, and one would only float on top. Here was a fix! Yet somehow I felt that though the boat seemed in a bad way, the master was watching even while he seemed to sleep, and help would surely come. In the darkness I stumbled across a huge shell-hole crater, recently made, with no water. Into it we rolled and lay on our faces, while the tempest howled around and angry shells hissed overhead and burst on every side. For a few moments I shivered with fear, for we were now right in the middle of the barrage and the danger was very great, but my courage came back when I remembered how easily he who had raised the tempest saved his apostles from it, and I never doubted he would do the same for us. Not a man was touched, though one had his rifle smashed to bits.

We reached head quarters, a strong block house made of concrete and iron rails, a masterpiece of German cleverness. From time to time all during the night the enemy gunners kept firing at our shelter, having the range to a nicety. Scores exploded within a few feet of it, shaking us till our bones rattled; a few went smash against the walls and roof, and one burst at the entrance nearly blowing us over, but doing no harm thanks to the scientific construction of the passage. I tried to get a few winks of sleep on a stool, there was no room to lie down with sixteen men in a small hut. And I came to the conclusion that so far we had not done badly and there was every promise of an exciting time.

6 August

The following morning, though the colonel and other officers pressed me very much to remain with them on the ground that I would be more comfortable, I felt I could do better work at the advanced dressing-station, or rather aid-post, and went and joined the doctor. It was a providential step and saved me from being the victim of an extraordinary accident. The following night a shell again rushed into the dug-out severely burning some and almost suffocating all the officers and men, fifteen in number, with poisonous fumes before they made their escape. Had I been there, I should have shared the same fate, so you can imagine what I felt as I saw all my friends carried off to hospital, possibly to suffer ill effects for life, while I by the merest chance was left behind well and strong to carry on God's work. I am afraid you will think me ungrateful, but more than once I almost regretted my escape, so great had been the strain of these past days now happily over.

For once getting out of bed was an easy, in fact, delightful task, for I was stiff and sore from my night's rest. My first task was to look round and see what were the possibilities for Mass. As all the dug-outs were occupied if not destroyed or flooded, I was delighted to discover a tiny ammunition store which I speedily converted into a chapel, building an altar with the boxes. The fact that it barely held myself did not signify as I had no server and had to be both priest and acolyte, and in a way I was not sorry I could not stand up, as I was able for once to offer the holy sacrifice on my knees.

It is strange that out here a desire I have long cherished should be gratified, viz.: to be able to celebrate alone, taking as much time as I wished without inconveniencing anyone. I read long ago in the Acts of the Martyrs of a captive priest, chained to the floor of the Coliseum, offering up the Mass on the altar of his own bare breast, but apart from that, Mass that morning must have been a strange one in the eyes of God's angels, and I trust not unacceptable to him. Returning to the dressing station, I refreshed the inner man in preparation for a hard day's work. You may be curious to know what an aid-post is like. Get out of your mind all ideas of a clean hospital ward, for our first aid dressing station is any place, as near as possible to the fighting line, which will afford a little shelter: a cellar, a coal hole, sometimes even a shell-hole. Here the wounded who have been roughly bandaged on the field are brought by the stretcher bearers to be dressed by the doctor. Our aid-post was a rough tin shed built beside a concrete dug-out which we christened the Pig Sty. You could just crawl in on hands and knees to the solitary chamber which served as a dressing room, recreation hall, sleeping apartment and anything else you cared to use it for. One could not very well sit up much less stand in our chateau, but you could stretch your legs and get a snooze if the German shells and the wounded men let you. On the floor were some wood shavings, kept well moistened in damp weather by a steady drip from the ceiling, and which gave covert to a host of curious little creatures, all most friendly and affectionate. There was room for three but as a rule we slept six or seven officers side by side. I had the post of honour next the wall, which had the double advantage of keeping me cool and damp, and of offering a stout resistance if anyone wanted to pinch more space, not an easy task, you may well conclude.

I spent a good part of the day, when not occupied with the wounded, wandering round the battle-field with a spade to bury stray dead. Though there was not very much infantry fighting owing to the state of the ground, not for a moment during the week did the artillery duel cease, reaching at times a pitch of unimaginable intensity. I have been through some hot stuff at Loos, and the Somme was warm enough for most of us, but neither of them could compare to the fierceness of the German fire here. For example, we once counted fifty shells, big chaps too, whizzing over our little nest in sixty seconds, not counting those that burst close by. In fact you became so accustomed to it all that you ceased to bother about them, unless some battery started strafing your particular position when you began to feel a keen personal interest in every new comer. I have walked about for hours at a time getting through my work, with crumps of all sizes bursting in dozens on every side.

More than once my heart has nearly jumped out of my mouth from sudden terror, but not once during all these days have I had what I could call a narrow escape, but always a strange confident feeling of trust and security in the all-powerful protection of our Blessed Lord. You will see before the end that my trust was not misplaced. All the same I am not foolhardy nor do I expose myself to danger unnecessarily, the coward is too strong in me for that; but when duty calls I know I can count on the help of one who has never failed me yet.

7 August 1917

No Mass this morning, thanks, I suppose, to the kindly attention of the evil one. I reached my chapel of the previous morning only to find that a big 9.5 inch shell had landed on the top of it during the day; went away feeling very grateful I had not been inside at the time, but had to abandon all thought of Mass as no shelter could be found from the heavy rain.

The battalion went out today for three days' rest, but I remained behind. Father Browne has gone back to the Irish Guards. He is a tremendous loss, not only to myself personally, but to the whole brigade where he did magnificent work and made a host of friends. And so I was left alone.

Another chaplain was appointed, but for reasons best known to himself he did not take over his battalion and let them go into the fight alone. There was nothing for it but to remain on and do his work, and glad I was I did so, for many a man went down that night, the majority of whom I was able to anoint.

Word reached me about midnight that a party of men had been caught by shell fire nearly a mile away. I dashed off in the darkness, this time hugging my helmet as the enemy was firing gas shells. A moment's pause to absolve a couple of dying men, and then I reached the group of smashed and bleeding bodies, most of them still breathing. The first thing I saw almost unnerved me; a young soldier lying on his back, his hands and face a mass of blue phosphorus flame, smoking horribly in the darkness. He was the first victim I had seen of the new gas the Germans are using, a fresh horror in this awful war. The poor lad recognised me, I anointed him on a little spot of unburnt flesh, not a little nervously, as the place was reeking with gas, gave him a drink which he begged for so earnestly, and then hastened to the others.

Back again to the aid-post for stretchers and help to carry in the wounded, while all the time the shells are coming down like hail. Good God! how can any human thing live in this? As I hurry back I hear that two men have been hit twenty yards away. I am with them in a moment, splashing through mud and water. A quick absolution and the last rites of the Church. A flash from a gun shows me that the poor boy in my arms is my own servant, or rather one who took the place of my orderly while he was away, a wonderfully good and pious lad.

By the time we reached the first party, all were dead, most of them with charred hands and faces. One man with a pulverised leg was still living. I saw him off to hospital made as comfortable as could be, but I could not help thinking of his torture as the stretcher jolted over the rough ground and up and down the shell holes.

Little rest that night, for the Germans simply pelted us with gas shells of every description, which, however, thanks to our new helmets, did no harm.

8 August 1917

There is little to record during the next couple of days except the discovery of a new cathedral and the happiness of daily Mass. This time I was not quite so well off, as I could not kneel upright and my feet were in the water which helped to keep the fires of devotion from growing too warm.

Having carefully removed an ancient German leg, I managed to vest by sitting on the ground, a new rubric I had to introduce also at the Communion, as otherwise I could not have emptied the chalice. I feel that when I get home again I shall be absolutely miserable because everything will be so clean and dry and comfortable. Perhaps some kind friend will pour a bucket or two of water over my bed occasionally to keep me in good spirits.

When night fell, I made my way up to a part of the line which could not be approached in daylight, to bury an officer and some men. A couple of grimy, unwashed figures emerged from the bowels of the earth to help me, but first knelt down and asked for absolution. They then leisurely set to work to fill in the grave. 'Hurry up, boys', I said. 'I don't want to have to bury you as well,' for the spot was a hot one. They both stopped working much to my disgust, for I was just longing to get away. 'Be gobs, Father,' replied one, I haven't the divil a bit of fear in me now after the holy absolution. 'Nor I, chimed in the other, I am as happy as a king.' The poor padre who had been keeping his eye on a row of crumps which were coming unpleasantly near felt anything but happy; however, there was nothing for it but to stick it out as the men were in a pious mood; and he escaped at last, grateful that he was not asked to say the Rosary.

10 August 1917

A sad morning as casualties were heavy and many men came in dreadfully wounded. One man was the bravest I ever met. He was in dreadful agony, for both legs had been blown off at the knee but never a complaint fell from his lips, even while they dressed his wounds, and he tried to make light of his injuries. 'Thank God, Father,' he said, 'I am able to stick it out to the end …' The extreme unction, as I have noticed time and again, eased his bodily pain. 'I am much better now and easier, God bless you,' he said, as I left him to attend a dying man. He opened his eyes as I knelt beside him: 'Ah! Fr Doyle, Fr Doyle,' he whispered faintly, and then motioned me to bend lower as if he had some message to give. As I did so, he put his two arms round my neck and kissed me. It was all the poor fellow could do to show his gratitude that he had not been left to die alone and that he would have the consolation of receiving the last sacraments before he went to God. Sitting a little way off I saw a hideous bleeding object, a man with his face smashed by a shell, with one if not both eyes torn out. He raised his head as I spoke. 'Is that the priest? Thank God, I am all right now.' I took his blood-covered hands in mine as I searched his face for some whole spot on which to anoint him. I think I know better now why Pilate said 'Behold the Man' when he showed our Lord to the people.

In the afternoon, while going my rounds, I was forced to take shelter in the dug-out of a young officer belonging to another regiment. He was a Catholic from Dublin, and had been married just a month. Was this a chance visit, or did God send me there to prepare him for death, for I had not long left the spot when a shell burst and killed him? I carried his body out the next day and buried him in a shell hole, and once again I blessed that protecting hand which had shielded me from his fate.

That night we moved headquarters and aid-post to a more advanced position, a strong concrete emplacement, but a splendid target for the German gunners. For the forty-eight hours we were there they hammered us almost constantly day and night till I thought our last hour had come. There we lived with a foot, sometimes more, of water on the floor, pretty well soaked through, for it was raining hard at times. Sleep was almost impossible – fifty shells a minute made some noise and to venture out without necessity was foolishness. We were well-provided with tinned food, and a spirit lamp for making hot tea, so that we were not too badly off, and rather enjoyed hearing the German shells hopping off the roof or bursting on the walls of their own strong fort.

11 August 1917

Close beside us I had found the remains of a dug-out which had been blown in the previous day and three men killed. I made up my mind to offer up Mass there for the repose of their souls. In any case I did not know a better hole to go to, and to this little act of charity I attribute the saving of my life later on in the day. I had barely fitted up my altar when a couple of shells burst overhead, sending the clay tumbling down. For a moment I felt very tempted not to continue as the place was far from safe. But later I was glad I went on for the Holy Souls certainly came to my aid as I did to theirs.

I had finished breakfast and had ventured a bit down the trench to find a spot to bury some bodies left lying there. I had reached a sheltered corner, when I heard the scream of a shell coming towards me rapidly, and judging by the sound, straight for the spot where I stood. Instinctively I crouched down,

and well I did so, for the shell whizzed past my head
I felt my hair blown about by the hot air and burst in
front of me with a deafening crash. It seemed to me
as if a heavy wooden hammer had hit me on the top
of the head, and I reeled like a drunken man, my ears
ringing with the explosion. For a moment I stood
wondering how many pieces of shrapnel had hit me,
or how many legs and arms I had left, and then dashed
through the thick smoke to save myself from being
buried alive by the shower of falling clay which was
rapidly covering me. I hardly know how I reached
the dug-out for I was speechless and so badly shaken
that it was only by a tremendous effort I was able to
prevent myself from collapsing utterly as I had seen
so many do from shell shock. Then a strange thing
happened: something seemed to whisper in my ear,
one of those sudden thoughts which flash through the
mind: Did not that shell come from the hand of God?
He willed it should be so. Is it not a proof that he can
protect you no matter what the danger?

The thought that it was all God's doing acted like
a tonic; my nerves calmed down, and shortly after I
was out again to see could I meet another iron friend.
As a matter of fact I wanted to see exactly what had
happened, for the report of a high explosive shell is
so terrific that one is apt to exaggerate distances. An
officer recently assured me he was only one foot from
a bursting shell, when in reality he was a good forty
yards away. You may perhaps find it hard to believe,

as I do myself, what I saw. I had been standing by a trellis work of thin sticks. By stretching out my hand I could touch the screen, and the shell fell smashing the woodwork! My escape last year at Loos was wonderful, but then I was some yards away, and partly protected by a bend in the trench. Here the shell fell, I might say, at my very feet; there was no bank, no protection except the wall of your good prayers and the protecting arm of God.

That night we were relieved, or rather it was early morning, 4.30 a.m., when the last company marched out. I went with them so that I might leave no casualties behind.

We hurried over the open as fast as we could, floundering in the thick mud, tripping over wires in the darkness. We had nearly reached the road, not knowing it was a marked spot when like a hurricane a shower of shells came smashing down upon us. We were fairly caught and for once I almost lost hope of getting through in safety. For five minutes or more we pushed on in desperation; we could not stop to take shelter, for dawn was breaking and we should have been seen by the enemy. Right and left, in front and behind, some far away, many very close, the shells kept falling Crash! One has pitched in the middle of the line, wounding five men, none of them seriously. Surely God is good to us, for it seems impossible a single man will escape unhurt, and then when the end seemed at hand, our batteries opened fire with a roar to support an attack that was beginning. The German guns ceased like magic, or turned their attention elsewhere, and we scrambled on to the road and reached home without further loss.

* * *

14 August 1917. Fr Doyle's last letter home; he had been killed by the time the letter was received
I have told you all my escapes, dearest father, because I think what I have written will give you the same confidence which I feel, that my old armchair up in heaven is not ready yet, and I do not want you to be uneasy about me. I am all the better for these couple of days rest, and am quite on my fighting legs again. Leave will be possible very shortly, I think, so I shall only say au revoir in view of an early meeting. Heaps of love to every dear one.

As ever, dearest father, your loving son,
Willie.

Fr Doyle was killed three days later. His body was never recovered.

Chapter Two:
The War Within

Father Doyle's heroism during nearly two years spent as a military chaplain has captured the imagination of many in the century since his death. But it was his secret, hidden life of prayer and penance, faithfully recorded in his private notebooks, that is perhaps the most surprising and inspiring aspect of his life and helps to make sense of his unselfish heroism at the front.

Father Doyle's notebooks were never intended to be read by others – he left a written request asking that they be destroyed in case of his death. However, his Jesuit superiors did not follow his request, and many details of Fr Doyle's spiritual life were published by Alfred O'Rahilly in his blockbuster biography in the 1920s. While the ethics of this may be questionable, it has been standard practice for the private diaries of many saints and holy people to be published in order to inspire and edify others. Most recently, for example, the private spiritual diaries of St John Paul II have been published in multiple languages, despite his request that they be kept hidden.

What we find in Fr Doyle's diaries is a firm, dedicated and dogged pursuit of holiness. Growth in virtue is hard, and he was no exception to this rule.

Writing in the late 1920s, fellow Jesuit Fr Hugh Kelly described Fr Doyle's notes in this way:

> By means of these papers, which were never meant for publication … we can watch him at work, as we can watch an artist in his studio. The blurred, generous aspirations of his early life towards sanctity, which acquire clearness of outline and direction only after years of effort, the frequent resolutions, the little failures, the human weakness, the generosity of soul … they are all laid bare in these private journals … They show us that most rare and instructive sight – sanctity in the making.

If we wonder how a boy from a privileged middle-class background, who had doubtful health all his life, and who had a nervous breakdown as a result of being caught up in a fire around the age of twenty, could mature into an unshakeable source of strength and serenity for his 'poor brave boys' in the war, we need look no further than the daily efforts to discipline himself and pursue holiness that is revealed in these diaries. We cannot have the heroic Willie Doyle of the trenches without the heroic Willie Doyle at prayer and penance – one grew naturally from the other.

Some contextual background may assist in understanding his private spiritual writings. Saint Ignatius of Loyola, the founder of the Jesuits, a mystic himself, encouraged a methodical approach to prayer for beginners in the spiritual life and life-long commitment to the examination of conscience. In the Spiritual Exercises, written as a guide to those on the path to deeper conversion, he advised two examinations of conscience per day – a particular examination at lunch time which is aimed at overcoming the person's particularly troublesome dominant defect, and a more general examination of the entire day before retiring for the night. He advised making notes on these examinations in order to monitor progress and to act as a warning against slipping back into bad habits, as well as reflecting on prayer in order to take note of where the Holy Spirit seemed to be prompting the one praying and to make further progress in prayer. Adopting this approach to the spiritual life can easily evolve into the habit of what we might today call 'journalling'. Father Doyle, like many religious of his day, especially other Jesuits, kept very detailed notes about his prayer and struggle for virtue in order to assist his progress. These private notes reveal two key aspects of his spiritual life.

The first is an intense life of prayer and union with God. He writes often about how he longs to be alone to pray, but has so much work on his hands and cannot find the time, and must often abandon sleep in order to seek that silence with God that he craved. One striking feature of this prayer is that he perceived that God was directly communicating with his soul, giving him particular messages or inspirations. Father Doyle was not the recipient of 'visions' per se, but he nevertheless had a strong sense of union with God and of the particular path God wanted him to follow. He studied for sixteen years before his ordination and was an avid reader of books on spirituality and the lives of the saints. He was a renowned spiritual director, who also consulted other experienced spiritual directors internationally. He was a practical and efficient man of affairs who was well-travelled, loved sports and inspired ordinary workers and soldiers. One of his dominant characteristics was his cheerfulness and love of good jokes. These characteristics do not suggest a man who is easily lead astray by his imagination.

The second aspect of Fr Doyle's life revealed in his diaries is his attraction to a life of penance and hardship offered particularly in reparation for the sins of priests. His private notes, and the advice he gave to others, make it abundantly clear that he believed this to be a specific calling for him personally and was not to be imitated by others. He felt this as a persistent force over many years – it was not a fleeting thought. He believed that activities and comforts that were perfectly appropriate for other people, including other priests, were not the path he was called to walk. He had approval from his Jesuit superiors for his plan of life. His advice to others was to do their ordinary duty well, and adopt very small penances, the smaller the better so long as they are motivated by love.

He himself, however, in fidelity to what he experienced as an inner call, practised often severe physical penances familiar from age-old Christian tradition and the lives of many saints. A generation as obsessed as ours is with gyms, weights and jogging might have some understanding of what St Paul wrote in the first century to the Corinthians about their athletic preoccupations:

Every athlete exercises self-control in all things. They do it to receive a perishable wreath, but we an imperishable. Well, I do not run aimlessly, I do not box as one beating the air; but I pommel my body and subdue it, lest after preaching to others I myself should be disqualified. (1 Corinthians 9: 25-27).

Willie Doyle's motivation, like that of the saints he so desired to emulate, was not only to strengthen his will in the daily battle against the body's unruly appetites but also, again like them, more mystically, to make reparation for his own sins and the sins of others. As St Paul wrote to the Colossians, 'Now I rejoice in my sufferings for your sake, and in my flesh I complete what is lacking in Christ's afflictions for the sake of his body, that is, the church.' (1:24).

This brief selection from Fr Doyle's private spiritual notes covers a number of common themes. Firstly, we see his burning desire for holiness and growth in the love of God, and his willingness to do whatever it took to be who he felt God wanted him to be, even to the point of becoming a martyr. Gradually this desire takes a particular form – the perception that God is calling him to a particular life of self-discipline and the denial of comfort, especially offered up for priests. We can then see how that manifested itself in his disciplined application to his daily work, as well as to the use of food and sleep. Finally, even in the trenches, we see his efforts to fight against what he came to see as his main defect – impatience – by placing himself at the disposal of others, whoever they might be, and making himself the 'slave' of all.

The brave chaplain of the trenches was shaped and formed over many years; he was not born that way. Part of the secret of his transformation is laid bare for us to see in these notes.

Growing desire for holiness and realisation of his 'call' to a hard life

28 July 1907, Milltown Park, Dublin: Fr Doyle's ordination day

My loving Jesus, on this the morning of my ordination to the priesthood, I wish to place in your Sacred Heart, in gratitude for all You have done for me, the resolution from this day forward *to go straight for holiness.* My earnest wish and firm resolve is to strive with might and main to become a saint.

Retreat 1909

I feel within me a constant desire or craving for holiness, a longing for prayer and a great attraction for mortification. Even walking along the streets I feel God tugging at my heart and, in a sweet loving way, urging, urging, urging me to give myself up absolutely to him and his service. Over and over again I say, 'My God, I will become a saint since you ask it.' But there is no progress, no real effort. The truth is, I am afraid of the sacrifice, afraid of doing what God wants; and I delude myself into thinking I am doing God's will and satisfying him by an empty promise. What an abuse of grace! This cannot go on. I feel there must be a change now in this retreat, an absolute surrender to all God wants.

22 January 1911

My dear loving Jesus, what do you want from me? You never seem to leave me alone – thank you ever so much for that – but keep on asking, asking, asking. I have tried to do a good deal lately for you and have made many little sacrifices which have cost me a good deal, but you do not seem to be satisfied with me yet and want more.

The same thought is ever haunting me, coming back again and again; fight as I will, I cannot get away from it or conceal from myself what it is you really want. I realise it more and more every day. But, my sweet Jesus, I am so afraid, I am so cowardly, so fond of myself and my own comfort, that I keep hesitating and refusing to give in to you and to do what you want.

Let me tell you what I think this is. You want me to immolate myself to your pleasure; to become your victim by self-inflicted suffering; to crucify myself in every way I can think of; never if possible to be without some pain or discomfort; to die to myself and to my love of ease and comfort; to give myself the necessaries of life but no more (and I think these could be largely reduced without injury to my health); to crucify my body in every way I can think of, bearing heat, cold, little sufferings, without relief, constantly, if possible always, wearing some instrument of penance; to crucify my appetite by trying to take as little delicacies as possible; to crucify my eyes by a vigilant guard over them; to crucify my will by submitting it to others; to give up all comfort, all self-indulgence; to sacrifice my love of ease, love for sleep at unusual times; to work, to toil for souls, to suffer, to pray always. My Jesus, am I not right, is not this what you want from me and have asked so long?

For the thought of such a life, so naturally terrifying, fills me with joy, for I know I could not do one bit of it myself but that it will all be the work of your grace and love. I have found, too, that the more I give, the more I do, the more I suffer, the greater becomes this longing.

Jesus, you know my longing to become a saint. You know how much I thirst to die a martyr. Help me to prove that I am really in earnest by living this life of martyrdom.

O loving Jesus, help me now not to fight any longer against you. I really long to do what you want, but I know my weakness so well and my inconstancy. I have made so many generous resolutions which I have never kept that I feel it is almost a mockery to promise more. This record of my feelings and desire at this moment will be a spur to my generosity; and if I cannot live up to the perfection of what you want, at least I am now determined to do more than I have ever done before. Help me, Jesus!

5 February 1911
Today while praying in the chapel, suddenly it seemed to me as if I were standing before a narrow path all choked with briars and sharp thorns. Jesus was beside me with a large cross and I heard him ask me would I strip myself of all things, and naked as he was on Calvary, take that cross on my bare shoulders and bravely fight my way to the end of the road. I realised clearly that this would mean much suffering and that very soon my flesh would be torn and bleeding from the thorns. All the same, humbly I promised him, that, relying on his grace, I would not shrink from what he asked, and even begged him to drag me through these briars since I am so cowardly. This inspiration, coming

so soon after the ardent desire really to crucify myself, shows me clearly what kind of life Jesus is asking from me. I felt impelled to resolve as far as possible never to be without some slight bodily suffering, e.g. chain on arm, etc ... All this has given me great interior peace and happiness, with fresh courage and determination to become a saint. Life is too short for a truce.

10 March 1911

This morning during meditation I again felt that mysterious appeal from our Blessed Lord for a life of absolute, complete sacrifice of every comfort. I see and feel now, without a shadow of a doubt, as certainly as if Jesus himself appeared and spoke to me, that he wants me to give up now and for ever all self-indulgence, to look on myself as not being free in the matter. That being so how can I continue my present manner of life, of a certain amount of generosity, fervent one day and then the next day giving in to self in everything?

When a little unwell, or when I have a slight headache. I lie down, give up work, indulge myself in the refectory. I see that I lose immensely by this, for that is the time of great merit, and Jesus sends me that pain to bear for him.

September 1911

If I were put in a dungeon, like the martyrs, with nothing to lie on but the bare stone floor, with no protection from intense cold, bread and water once a day for food, with no home comfort whatever, I could endure all that for years and gladly for the love of Jesus, yet I am unwilling to suffer a little inconvenience now, I must have every comfort, warm clothes, fire, food as agreeable as I possibly can, etc...

Sanctity is so precious, it is worth paying any price for it ... God sanctifies souls in many ways, the path of daily and hourly sacrifices in everything and always is mine.

10 July 1913
Last night I rose at two o'clock, very much against my will, and went down to the domestic chapel. Jesus seemed to want me to come before him as a victim of his divine anger on behalf of sinners ... Then he spoke in my soul clearly and forcibly: 'You must be your own executioner. I want you to sacrifice all, which you have never done yet though you often promised. From this hour you must never give yourself one grain of human comfort or self-indulgence even at the times you have been accustomed to do so, e.g. when very tired, not well, travelling, etc. I want from you a suffering love always, always, always. The feasts and relaxations of others are not for you. Give me this courageously and I will grant the desires of your heart.'

Jesus seemed to ask the following: (1) perfect denial of the eyes, (2) the bearing of little pains, (3) much prayer for strength, (4) a review of each half day at examen to see if this resolution has been kept.

My whole soul shrank from this life – 'no human comfort ever'. But with his grace, for I know my own weakness too well, I promised to do all he asked, and lying on the ground, I asked him to nail me to my cross and never again permit me to come down from it.

8 May 1914

My way is sure. I think I can say now without a shade of doubt or hesitation that the path by which Jesus wants me to walk is that of absolute abandonment of all human comfort and pleasure and the embracing as far as I can of every discomfort and pain ... How often does he not seem to say to me in prayer, 'I would have you strip yourself of all things – every tiny particle of self-indulgence, and this ever and always? Give me all and I will make you a great saint.' This then is the price of my life-long yearning for sanctification. O Jesus, I am so weak, help me to give you all and to do it now.

11 October 1914

Jesus told me at exposition, and I do not think that I have mistaken his voice, that the way in which I must sanctify myself is by suffering, corporal penance, and denial in all things.

22 November 1914

My big regret at death will be to have given in to self

so much, to have taken life to easily, and wasted so much time … and not to have slaved more for God's glory.

Reparation for the sins of priests
8 December 1915
I believe that Our Lord is asking for victims who are willing to suffer much in reparation for sins, especially those of priests.

15 October 1914
Last night I rose at one a.m. and walked two miles bare footed in reparation for the sins of priests to the chapel at Murrough [County Clare], where I made the Holy Hour. God made me realise the merit of each step, and I understood better how much I gain by not reading the paper; each picture, each sentence sacrificed means additional merit. I felt a greater longing for self-inflicted suffering and a determination to do more.

1 December 1914
The great light of this retreat, clear and persistent has been that God has chosen me, in his great love and through compassion for my weakness and misery, to be a victim of reparation for the sins of priests especially; that hence my life must be different in the matter of penance, self-denial and prayer, from the lives of others not given this special grace – they may meritoriously do what I cannot; that unless I

constantly live up to the life of a willing victim, I shall not please our Lord nor ever become a saint – it is the price of my sanctification; that Jesus asks this from me always and in every lawful thing, so that I can sum up my life 'sacrifice always in all things'.

28 July 1917, the tenth anniversary of his ordination and less than three weeks before his death. It was the last entry in his private diary.

I have again offered myself to Jesus as his victim to do with me absolutely as he pleases. I will try to take all that happens, no matter from whom it comes, as sent to me by Jesus and will bear suffering, heat cold, etc with joy as part of my immolation in reparation for the sins of priests. From this day I shall try bravely to bear all little pains in this spirit.

Daily duties

7 June 1907

While making the Holy Hour today ... I felt inspired to make this resolution: Sweet Jesus, as a first step towards my becoming a saint, which you desire so much, I will try to do each duty, each little action, as perfectly and fervently as I possibly can.

Retreat in 1909

It seems to me the best and most practical resolution I can make in this retreat is to determine to perform each action with the greatest perfection. This will mean a constant 'going against self' at every moment and every single day. I have a vast field to cover in my ordinary daily actions, e.g. to say the Angelus always with the utmost attention and fervour. I feel, too, that Jesus asks this from me, as without it there can be no real holiness.

February 1911[17]
Kneeling there I asked her what God wanted from me, when I heard an interior voice clearly repeating, 'Love him, love him.' The following day she seemed to rebuke me, when leaving the cemetery, for the careless

------

17. This incident occurred when Fr Doyle visited the grave of Ellen Organ, popularly known as 'Little Nellie of Holy God'. Ellen Organ was born in Waterford in 1903 and died in Cork 1908. Her mother died in 1907, and Ellen was placed in the care of the Good Shepherd sisters in Cork. She suffered from spinal injuries and spent much of her time in the infirmary, eventually dying of tuberculosis aged four and a half. She was noted for a very unusual early piety and longed to receive Holy Communion, despite being far too young to do so. She claimed to have had mystical experiences and visions. Following an investigation by a Jesuit priest, the local bishop agreed that she had in fact reached the age of reason and gave approval for Ellen to receive Holy Communion, and she did so thirty-two times before her death. She spent many hours in prayer each day, and after her death her fame spread globally. Several books have been written about her. When St Pius X heard of her story he requested a relic of her, and her life was instrumental in his decision to lower the age at which children receive their first Holy Communion. There is some discussion about her cause for beatification being initiated.

way I performed most of my spiritual duties, and to say that God was displeased with this and wanted great fervour and perfection in them.

The struggle with food

1 September 1911

I feel a growing thirst for self-denial; it is a pleasure not to taste the delicacies provided for me. I wish I could give up the use of meat entirely. I long even to live on bread and water. My Jesus, what marvellous graces you are giving me, who always have been so fond of eating and used to feel a small act of denial of my appetite a torture.

October 1911, while giving a retreat to Carmelite nuns

I felt urged in honour of St Teresa to give myself absolutely no comfort at meals which I could possibly avoid. I found no difficulty in doing this for the nine days. I have begged very earnestly for the grace to continue this all my life and am determined to try to do so. For example, to take no butter[18], no sugar

---

18. Father Doyle fought a long battle to give up butter and eat dry bread. It is fascinating to see those daily struggles over something that appears so trivial. But it is in such small matters that the will is disciplined and strengthened. St Josemaria Escriva, the founder of Opus Dei, read a Spanish translation of the life of Fr Doyle in 1933 and was impressed with what he termed the 'butter tragedy', and wrote about it in the following terms in his famous book *The Way*: We were reading – you and

in coffee, no salt, etc. The wonderful mortified lives of these holy nuns have made me ashamed of my gratification of my appetite.

18 September 1913
A fierce temptation during Mass and thanksgiving to break my resolution and indulge my appetite at breakfast. The thought of a breakfast of dry bread and tea without sugar in future seemed intolerable. Jesus urged me to pray for strength though I could scarcely bring myself to do so. But the temptation left me in the refectory, and joy filled my heart with the victory. I see now that I need never yield if only I pray for strength.

September 1913
God has been urging me strongly all during this retreat to give up butter entirely. I have done so at many meals without any serious inconvenience; but I am partly held back through human respect, fearing others may notice it. If they do, what harm?… One thing I feel Jesus asks, which I have not the courage to give him – the promise to give up butter entirely.

I – the heroically ordinary life of that man of God. And we saw him fight whole months and years (what 'accounts' he kept in his particular examination!) at breakfast time: today he won, tomorrow he was beaten … He noted: 'Didn't take butter …; did take butter!' May you and I too live our 'butter tragedy'.

22 February 1914

Jesus taught me a simple way today of conquering the temptation to break resolutions. When, for example, I want to take sugar in my tea, etc., I will make a vow[19] not to do so for that one occasion, which will compel me to do it, no matter what it may cost. I know often I shall have to force myself to take this little vow; but I realise that if only I can bring myself to say 'I vow,' then all the conflict raging in my soul about that particular thing will cease at once. This will be invaluable to me in the future.

Undated but from the front

No blackberries. Give away all chocolates. Give away box of biscuits. No jam, breakfast, lunch, dinner.

Denial of sleep and prayer at night

1 September 1911

Last night while making the Holy Hour in my room, Jesus seemed to ask me to promise to make it every Thursday, even when away giving retreats, and when

---

19. Mother Teresa of Calcutta, canonised in 2016, was familiar with the life of Fr Doyle, probably from her contact with Jesuit spiritual directors who promoted his life and spirituality. She personally adopted Fr Doyle's practice of making short temporary vows in this way. Mother Teresa was also influenced by St Therese of Lisieux, and Sr Benigna Consolata, an Italian nun who died in 1916, who both also made vows of this nature.

I cannot go to the chapel, he wants the greater part of the time to be spent prostrate on the ground, which I find very painful. I think he wants me to share in his agony during this hour, feeling a little of the sadness, desolation, and abandonment he experienced, the shame of sin, the uselessness of his sufferings to save souls. I begged him to plunge my soul into the sea of bitterness which surrounded him. It was an hour of pain, but I hope for more.

12 May 1913
I find the temptation growing stronger every day to leave aside all work that is not absolutely necessary and to spend the time with Jesus. Why does he make me realise so much his loneliness in the tabernacle and his longing for 'one to console him,' and at the same time fill my hands with so many things to do? ... These moments before him are rich in grace, especially recently, and I find it hard to think of anything but Jesus and his love.

22 January 1915
Last night I rose at twelve and knelt in the cellar for an hour to suffer from the cold. It was a hard fight to do so, but Jesus helped me. I said my Rosary with arms extended. At the third mystery the pain was so great that I felt I could not possibly continue; but at each Hail Mary I prayed for strength and was able to finish it. This has given me great consolation by

showing the many hard things I could do with the help of prayer.

12 July 1915

Not feeling well, I gave up the intention of sleeping on boards, but overcame self and did so. I rose this morning quite fresh and none the worse for it, proving once more how our Lord would help me if I were generous.

25 October 1916

Jesus has long urged me to give Him a whole night of prayer and reparation. Last night I prayed in my dug-out at Kemmel from nine till five (eight hours), most of the time on my knees … Though I had only two hours' sleep, I am not very tired or weary today. Jesus wants more of these nights of prayer, adoration and atonement.

To be the slave of all

February 1916

Reading today of how Luisa de Caravajal[20] made

---

20. Luisa de Caravajal was a Spanish noblewoman who lived in London and who died in 1614. She was especially close to the persecuted Jesuits who ministered there and knew many of the martyrs of the Elizabethan persecution. Father Doyle had a strong personality and his biggest defect may have been his tendency towards impatience. Saint Ignatius recommends that dominant defects like this can best be tackled by 'acting against' them. Father Doyle seems to have decided that the best way to

herself the slave of her two maids, the old desire for this kind of life sprang up again.

13 October 1916
Lately the desire to be trampled on and become the slave of everybody has grown very strong. I have resolved to make myself secretly the slave of my servant[21], and, as far as I can, to submit to his will e.g. to wait till he comes to serve my Mass and not to send for him, never to complain of anything he does, to take my meals in the way he chooses to cook them and at the hours he suggests, to let him arrange things in the way he sees fit, in a word humbly to let him trample on me as I deserve.

---

overcome his own impatience was to act as if he was the slave of others – to deliberately put others first and to do what they asked.

21. Fr Doyle had the rank of Captain in the army and thus had an orderly or servant to assist him with material concerns. He seems to have had much to suffer at the hands of his orderly. From Fr Frank Browne SJ: 'I rode over one morning to see Fr Doyle. I found him writing letters, which he interrupted to tell me of Murphy's latest. Pointing to his trench boots he asked me to smell them. They were awful. Murphy, in order to prepare them for polishing, had in the orthodox way washed them, but in an unorthodox manner he had chosen a cesspool! The result was almost too much for Fr Willie. When I told him to sack Murphy on the spot, saying that it was getting a bit too much of a good joke, he laughed and said: 'Well, he's a decent poor fellow and he means well; and – well, perhaps I can gain something too'.

26 October 1916

I am slowly learning the lesson Jesus brought me out here to teach me. The first and greatest is that I must have no will of my own, only his, and this in all things. It is hard to let everyone walk on you, even your own servant; but Jesus asks this and I try to let him arrange all as he pleases. Result: yesterday I got no dinner, though I foresaw this would be the consequence of this planning.

22 December 1916

My genius of an orderly fried meat and pudding together and, with a smile of triumph on his face, brought both on the same plate to my dug-out. He is a good poor chap, but I would not recommend him as a cook.

22 May 1917

I hear Michael, my orderly, hard at work frying onions for my dinner, what a time we are going to have ... I am hoping for great things and that he won't wash my socks again in the water with which he makes the tea. After all as the farmer says 'pigs is pigs and war is war' and fresh water is scarce, so hurrah for the laundry tea!

Chapter Three:
Spiritual Advice

In addition to being a well-known preacher and retreat master, Fr Doyle was regularly sought out as a spiritual director and adviser, often receiving dozens of letters each day seeking his insights. A selection of his meditations and spiritual advice is presented under a variety of alphabetically arranged themes. In addition to providing an insight into Fr Doyle's own spirituality, some of these points could also be useful for personal prayer.

Abandonment to Divine Providence

Abandon yourself completely into the hands of God, and take directly from him every event of life, agreeable, or disagreeable. Only then can God make you really holy.

He loves your soul dearly, cling to him, and trust him, he so longs to be trusted.

I would like you to know what I think Jesus wants from you. He would like you to place yourself in his hands entirely, giving him full permission to do what he likes with you. Thus you will accept lovingly crosses, trials, joys and sickness, which you will try to take from his loving hands as a proof of love. Don't ask for suffering, but open your arms wide if it comes.

Accepting ourselves

You must have great patience with yourself and not expect to get into a region of perfect peace where there would be no trials or worries or fighting against self – even the saints did not enjoy that calm.

Remember, God sees the intention, which in your case is generous and unreserved. He is quite pleased with that, and only smiles when he sees us failing in our resolve and determination to be perfect. To console you, here is the confession of the great St Teresa: 'The devil sends me so offensive a spirit of bad temper that at times I think I could eat people up.' She was canonised, so there is some hope of salvation for us yet.

Don't dwell on what you have not done, for I think that want of confidence in his willingness to forgive our shortcomings pains him very much, but rather lift up your heart and think what you are going to do for him now.

Angels

He hath given his angels charge over us, to guide us, to guard and shelter us from dangers, to lead us safely through this world of sin and bring us to the throne prepared for us in heaven. Ever beside us our faithful angel stays. We heed him not; his spotless purity, his majestic dignity, checks us not in our career of sin; but could we see our guardian spirit when passion urges us on, the sight would check our downward path.

Apostolate

'They forgot God who saved them.' (Psalm 106: 21). To how many may not these words be applied today! How many there are who come into this world and pass beyond its bounds and never know the loving God who died to save them.

God has work for each one to do; the devil also. For each one can be an influence for good or evil to those around. No one goes to heaven or hell alone.

Are you weary of the fight already and willing to give in to the enemy? Never mind, come back, begin again, Jesus wants you. There are millions of pagans to be saved, a hundred thousand dying sinners every day to be rescued. For shame, to sit down and cry over your own self and troubles while so many others need your aid.

Begin again

I am convinced from a pretty big experience that perfection, that is sanctity, is only to be won by repeated failures. If you rise again after a fall, sorry for the pain given to our Lord, humbled by it since you see better your real weakness, and determined to make another start, far more is gained than if you had gone on without a stumble.

'Begin again' is the motto of success in the path of holiness. Remember, too, that faults and falls rightly used help to teach us our weakness and to make us humble, and so are really a stepping-stone to greater sanctity.

Perseverance is what God wants. If we get up and start again after each fall, God will make saints of us in the end.

When you commit a fault which humbles you and for which you are really sorry, it is a gain instead of a loss.

A frequent prayer of the saints must have been, I think: 'Failed again, Lord, I'll begin again.'

Cheerfulness

Keep smiling. It is a grand thing to cultivate a smile. Keep the corners of your mouth up, especially if you are in for an attack of the dumps. There are three Ds to be avoided: the Devil, the Doctor, and the Dumps. The Devil, we all know, is bad enough; the Doctor is very little better; and the Dumps are the Devil himself! So I repeat, keep smiling, it is the very best remedy for gloom. The devil loves nothing better than a gloomy soul; it is his plaything.

You must absolutely drive away all despondency or useless pining or regrets about the past. It does not please God and it only injures your spiritual life.

Children of God

We are all God's children, fashioned by his divine hands after his own image and likeness. From all eternity he has thought of us; before time was, we were present to his mind; and through the long ages which have passed away since first this world was made, God busied himself with our creation; has longed for the hour when he could call us his children.

The more lowly, humble and childlike you are, the more will you win the love and affection of Jesus. I wonder that we do not think more on his clear teaching about sanctity: unless you become as a child, you will never be a saint.

Complaining

'Oh, my God, I will never complain.' You will get to heaven by keeping this one resolution, 'Never to complain.' We are always rebelling or inclined to rebel. Oh! How few are the exceptions to this sweeping accusation. We are all of us inclined to rebel, and most of us do rebel, and are perpetually rebelling. We forget the little compact that God enters into with all of us. It is this he says to each one of us, 'My child, walk on submissively in your few years of trial here, and, in reward of your obedience to my will, I will bestow on you an eternity of happiness.' This compact really exists; it has been made with everyone of us. How beautifully St Paul alludes to it: 'For I reckon,' he says, 'that the sufferings of this time are not to be compared with the glory to come, that shall be revealed to us.' We are pleased with this compact of our dearest Lord; it shows his love and tenderness for us. But, base cowards that we are, in place of walking on bravely in our thorny path, we are perpetually complaining. No! Not one in ten thousand pays attention to this little compact; hence we find all complaining, *except saints*. Nuns complain. Priests complain. Monks complain. All complain, except God's true servants, and these 'never complain', for they understand God's simple little compact which I have stated above. Well, then, tell God you will 'never complain'. This one resolution will stop up all outbursts of temper, all uncharitableness. It will make our interior calm and patient, like our divine Lord himself.

Confession

I, too, used long ago to hate Confession, for no reason whatever, till as a priest I began to realise the fact that it is the biggest help and quickest means to holiness, since a sacrament pours grace into the soul ... Go every day if you can.

Daily duties

Each fresh meditation on the life of our Lord impresses on me more and more the necessity of conforming my life to his in every detail if I wish to please him and become holy. To do something great and heroic may never come, but I can make my life heroic by faithfully and daily putting my best effort into each duty as it comes round.

Each succeeding hour brings with it some allotted task, yet in the faithful performance of these trifling acts of our everyday life lies the secret of true sanctity.

I am truly glad you are looking to the perfection of your daily actions; it is the simplest, yet perhaps hardest, way of sanctification, with little fear of deception. It is the certain following of Christ: 'He hath done all things well.' (Mark 7: 37).

Divine Mercy

Jesus during his mortal life practised many virtues; but none is more conspicuous; none appeals more strongly to us, than his infinite mercy, his tender forgiveness of all injuries.

Eucharist

Try basking in the sun of God's love, that is, quietly kneeling before the tabernacle, as you would sit enjoying the warm sunshine, not trying to do anything except love him; but realising that, during all the time you are at his feet, more especially when dry and cold, grace is dropping down upon your soul and you are growing fast in holiness.

The closer I try to imitate the Sacred Heart, the holier shall I become. How can I get nearer that divine heart than by receiving Holy Communion often and fervently? The Sacred Heart will then be next my own and will teach me quickest and best how to be a saint.

Do we realise the infinite possibilities of grace which lie hidden in the Tabernacle? Jesus only awaits our coming; and even before we have begun to beg his help, he has opened the treasures of his Sacred Heart and filled our hands with priceless gifts. What monarch ever rewarded his subjects as Jesus repays us for the little trouble it costs us to visit him even for one short moment?

As a means of gaining greater recollection, each morning at Holy Communion invite Jesus to dwell in your heart during the day as in a tabernacle. Try all day to imagine even his bodily presence within you and often turn your thoughts inwards and adore him as he nestles next to your heart in a very real manner … This habit is not easily acquired, especially in a busy life like yours, but much may be done by constant effort.

Family

'The good shepherd giveth his life for his sheep' (John 10: 1). And you, wives and bread winners, have you no task within the fold, no little flock to tend and guard? Has not God committed to your care the innocent lambs, the little ones of your household? Within the pasture of your own family are you the good shepherd, or the thief and the hireling? … Jesus does not ask from his shepherds now the shedding of their life-blood. But he does ask from them a death more hard, more lingering, a life-long death of sacrifice for his flock … the daily crucifying of every evil passion, the stamping out of sloth, of anger, of drunkenness, the constant striving after the holiness of their state of life …

If we want our work for souls to be fruitful, we must bring prayer into it. If our children are not all that they ought to be, the cause may not be far to seek. Let us examine if we are praying enough for them, if our aspirations are ever ascending to the throne of God, to bless our work amongst those children and amongst others with whom we have to deal.

Generosity

Live for the day, as you say but let it be a generous day. Have you ever tried giving God one day in which you refused him nothing, a day of absolute generosity?

Don't be one of those who give God everything but one little corner of their heart on which they put up a notice board with the inscription: 'Trespassers not allowed.'

Sanctity is so precious, it is worth paying any price for it…Will Jesus be content with only half-measures from me? I feel he will not; he asks for all. My Jesus, with your help I will give you all.

Be generous with him and he will be so with you … If you are faithful to God he will place his loving arms around you and hold you tight. Put away all fear in this regard; a soul in fear cannot be united to God. Trust, trust, trust.

God's will

Holiness is really nothing more than perfect conformity to God's will, and so every step in this direction must please him immensely.

How often have we murmured against the good God because he has refused our petitions or frustrated our plans? Can we look into the future as God can do?

Can we see now and realise to the full the effect our request would have had if granted? God loves us, he loves us too dearly to leave us to the guidance of our poor judgements; and when he turns a deaf ear to our entreaties, it is as a tender father would treat the longings of a child for what would work him harm.

We do not mind what God does with us so long as it more or less fits in with our own wishes; but when his will clashes with ours, we begin to see the difficulty of the prayer, 'Not my will but thine be done'.

Hard things

If one of two has to suffer, why shouldn't you be the one? Always choose the worst and the hardest. Do not try to get rid of what is troublesome or annoying, but hold on to it. The cross is a treasure.

Whenever there is a question of choice, ask yourself, 'Which would please God most?' then, 'Which will come hardest to my nature?' It is this then that you will choose; and even though you may not always do so, keep your mind and will bent in the direction of doing always whatever goes against self.

If I were put in a dungeon, like the martyrs, with nothing to lie on but the bare stone floor, with no protection from intense cold, bread and water once a day for food, with no home comfort whatever, I could endure all that for years and gladly for the love of Jesus; yet I am unwilling to suffer a little inconvenience now, I must have every comfort, warm clothes, fire, food as agreeable as I possibly can.

Going against self! Not in one thing or in two, but in all things where a free choice is left us. These little words contain the life-story of the saints, as they are the weapon that gained the victory which gave them heaven.

Holy Spirit

I sometimes think we lose very much by not having more devotion to the Holy Ghost. After all he is the dispenser of the very things we need to make us saints.

A devotion which does not consist in any special form of prayer nor in doing anything in particular more than to listen to inspirations, is devotion to the Holy Spirit of God. As the work of Creation belongs pre-eminently to the Father and that of redemption to the Son, so the work of our sanctification and perfection is the work of the Holy Ghost. We honour him when we listen to his inspirations.

He is ever whispering what we ought to do and what we ought not to do. When we are deliberately deaf to his voice, which is no other than the small voice of conscience, we grieve instead of honouring the Holy

Spirit of God. So let us often say: Come O Holy Ghost into my heart and make me holy so that I may be generous with God and become a saint. See what the Holy Spirit made of the apostles: changed them from skulking cowards into great saints afire with the love of God.

Humility
Creation implies two things, nothing and God. Strange combination! Yet man thinks much of himself. Let him sound the depths of his origin and he will find nothing.

There is one thing we need never be afraid of, namely, that the devil will ever tempt us to be humble. He may delude us in the practice of other virtues; indiscreet zeal, for instance, or the desire to devote our time solely to prayer. But we need never be in doubt as to whether it would be better to humble ourselves or not. There can be no doubt about it. It is always safe to do so.

Impatience
A sharp tongue is the only edged tool that grows sharper with use.

Crush at once every movement of impatience, that your soul may be always calm and not over-anxious.

Last things – death, judgement, purgatory, heaven, hell

Death

Pray for all, but especially for sinners, and in particular for those whose sins are most painful to his Sacred Heart. With great earnestness recommend to his mercy the poor souls who are in their agony. What a dreadful hour, an hour tremendously decisive, is the hour of our death! Surround with your love these souls going to appear before God, and defend them by your prayers.

Judgement

'Render an account of thy stewardship!' (Luke 16:2). To all of us these words must yet be spoken. Shall we hear them from the lips of an angry God, words full of awful menace for the treasures which we have squandered? Will they come to us in gentle reproach from a loving master, in tones of meek rebuke for a life of wasted opportunities? Or will this summons fill our hearts with holy joy, that now the world may see and know how well we have kept our trust, how faithfully served, how generously toiled for him who gave us all? Or what will be our feelings when too late the thought of all we might have done for Jesus will burst upon us? How little it would have cost us to have loved him more and served him better!

Purgatory

From their cleansing prison of fire the holy souls cry to us for help. With joy indeed they bear the pain which cleanses them from the foul marks of sin, for now at last they know the awful purity of him against whom on earth they dared to sin. Upon their souls they see the hideous taint of what was once their joy; and even were heaven's gates thrown open wide, they would not enter and stand with spotted robe before him in whose eyes the heavens themselves are not pure. Still they sigh and long for the happiness of their eternal home, for the company of the blessed saints, for Jesus whom at last they know. To be separated from him is now their most grievous pain, exceeding far the torture of the cleansing fires.

Heaven

When all is said and done, a man's religion is his biggest consolation, and the source of real courage. I reminded them of the saying of the (Saint) Curé d'Ars: 'When we get to Heaven and see all the happiness which is to be ours for ever, we shall wonder why we wanted to remain even one day on earth.' God hides these things from our eyes, for if we saw now 'the things God has prepared for those that love him' life on earth would be absolutely unliveable.

Hell

What would the damned not give for one moment of the time which we think so little of! If one of these unhappy souls could return again on earth and live again its ill-spent life, how differently it would look upon those things which before it despised? How eagerly it would gather up the fleeting moments that not one even might be lost, but each might bear its burden of mint into eternity. Would it have need, think you, of seeking useless amusements to pass the time? Would its days and years be swallowed up in the vain pursuit of useless trifles, its precious life squandered far from God in the evil haunts of sin? One moment of time for sorrow and repentance would turn the pit of hell into a paradise of delight.

Life of Christ

What impressed me most in the meditation on the Nativity was the thought that Jesus could have been born in wealth and luxury, or at least with the ordinary comforts of life, but he chose all that was hard, unpleasant and uncomfortable. This he did for me, to show me the life I must lead for him. If I want to be with Christ, I must lead the life of Christ, and in that life there was little of what was pleasing to nature. I think I have been following Christ, yet how pleasant and comfortable my life has always been; ever avoiding cold, hunger, hard work, disagreeable things, humiliations, etc. My Jesus, you are speaking to my heart now. I cannot mistake your voice or hide from myself what you want from me and what my future life should be. Help me for I am weak and cowardly.

I was greatly struck with the thought that at his birth, our Lord began a voluntary life of suffering which would never end till he died in agony on the cross. All this for me.

Great as was the poverty of Jesus in the cave at Bethlehem, it was nothing compared to his destitution during the flight into Egypt. Again this was voluntary and chosen and borne for me.

I should examine all my actions, taking Jesus as my model and example. What a vast difference between my prayer and his; between my use of time, my way of speaking, walking, dealing with others, etc., and that of the child Jesus! If I could only keep him before my eyes always, my life would be far different from what it has been.

Little things
Look upon nothing as too small to offer to God. Big sacrifices do not come very often, and generally we are too cowardly to make them when they do. But little ones are as plentiful as blackberries in September, and stiffen the moral courage, by the constant repetition of them, to do, in the end, even heroic things. Nothing

is too small; in fact the smaller it is the better, so long as it is some denial of your will, some act you would just as soon not do.

I think he would like you to pay more attention to little things, looking on nothing as small, if connected with his service and worship. Also try to remember that nothing is too small to offer to him.

Love of God

Recognise God's graces to you, and instead of thinking of yourself and your faults, try to do all you can for God, and love him more.

As the moth is attracted to the light, is drawn ever nearer to the warmth and brightness, until at length with irresistible longing it casts itself into the flame, so the Sacred Heart draws us to itself by its love. We are warmed by the fervour of its affection, dazzled by its brilliancy. We come to realise the extent of that love, its foolish excesses; it bursts upon us that all this is a personal love for me.

You can test your love infallibly and find out how much you have by asking yourself this question: What am I willing to suffer for him? It is the test of St Francis de Sales: 'Willingness to suffer is a certain proof of love.'

I think it is evident that, in these days of awful sin and hatred of God, our Blessed Lord wants to gather round him a legion of chosen souls who will be devoted, heart and soul, to him and his interests, and upon whom he may always count for help and consolation. Souls who will not ask 'How much must I do?' but rather 'How much can I do for his love?' A legion of souls who will give and not count the cost, whose only pain will be that they cannot do more and give more and suffer more for him who has done so much for them. In a word, souls who are not as the rest of men, fools perhaps in the eyes of the world, for their watchword is sacrifice and not self-comfort.

During the last few days the thought has come home to me that the truest title to address our divine Lord by is 'Poor Jesus'. He is rich in all things except the one he really cares about: the love of loving hearts.

We must love God with our whole heart. Can he be loved otherwise? Is it too much that a finite heart should love infinite beauty? I fail in this wholehearted love if I keep back anything from him, if I am determined not to pass certain limits as proof of my love, if I absolutely refuse to sacrifice certain things which he asks.

Mary

'Mother of Mercy!' What words more sweet in the sinner's ear! The past has been a long record of sin and sinfulness, of grace abused and calls neglected. God's inspirations have been despised, his patience abused, his anger defied. In terror the soul looks back on a misspent life; in horror it thinks of a judgement, just and searching, to come. How face the look of an angry God? How stand before him to whom nothing is hidden? How answer for the days and years squandered which were given to serve him alone? Oh! turn then, poor soul, and look to Mary. Look to her who is all merciful that she may obtain for you pardon and mercy. She is kind and loving; she has a mother's heart full of pity for the erring, a Mother of Mercy to the sinner and the fallen.

To Mary's feet in heaven today the angels come in never-ending stream to lay before her the offerings of her loving earthly children. To their queen they bear fair wreaths of lovely roses. In many a lonely cottage or amid the bustle of the great city have these crowns been formed. Little ones and old folk, the pious nun and holy priest, the sinner too and many a wandering soul, have added to the glory of the Queen of Heaven; and from every corner of this earth today has risen the joyous praise of her who is Queen of the Holy Rosary. On earth she was the lowly handmaid of the Lord, and now all generations proclaim the greatness of her name.

By her simple 'fiat' Mary brought to pass the most wondrous miracle of all time. In silent expectation the heavenly court had watched the great archangel speed on his way towards the humble home of Nazareth. With joy they heard the virgin's humble words of meek submission which brought the maker of the world to dwell within her womb, and now they see their God, the great God of all creatures dwelling as a little babe among sinful men.

What must have been Mary's thoughts when first she felt the infant child within her womb, and realised that from her pure blood he had fashioned to himself a human form? She his mother, he her son! What sweet converse between the two, what words of love, of ardent, tender love, the promptings of a heart so pure and good and holy.

God delights to honour his saints by bestowing upon them special graces which mark them off from the rest of mankind. To one he gives a burning zeal for souls; to another the thirst for suffering and humiliation, but on Mary alone he bestowed the supreme privilege of freedom from the taint of sin. From the first moment of her conception till she closed her eyes forever on this world, Mary was undefiled, unspotted by the least taint of sin. Never for an instant did the fierce and fiery burst of temptation ruffle the calm of her holy soul; for her the forbidden pleasures of this life, for which man will barter his priceless soul, had no false attraction. Sin might rage around her, hell might move its mighty depths, but nought could tarnish the spotless beauty of her who was to be the Mother of God.

Mass

What an inexhaustible reservoir of grace and endless sanctity is contained in the worthy celebration of or assistance at Mass. It seemed as if I were getting only drops instead of the torrents of grace and love which every Mass could bring to the soul.

Passion of Christ

During his passion our Lord was bound and dragged from place to place. I have hourly opportunities of imitating him by going cheerfully to the duty of the moment: recreation when I want to be quiet, a walk when I would rather stay in my room, some unpleasant duty I did not expect, a call of charity which means great inconvenience for myself.

During all these long years Jesus has been standing bound at the pillar, while I have cruelly scourged him by my ingratitude and neglect of my vocation. Each action carelessly done … each moment wasted, have been so many stripes on my saviour's bleeding body … And all the while I have heard his gentle voice, 'My child, will you not love me? I want your heart. I want you to strive and become a saint, to be generous with me and refuse me nothing.' Can I now turn away again as before and refuse to listen?

With Jesus naked and shivering with bitter cold at the pillar, I will try joyfully to bear the effects of cold. With Jesus covered with wounds I, too, will try to endure little sufferings without relief.

The greatest thirst of Jesus on the cross was his thirst for souls. He saw then the graces and inspirations he would give me to save souls for him. In what way shall I correspond and console my saviour?

Peace of heart

At all costs you must conquer and keep your peace of mind; otherwise goodbye to holiness.

Jesus knows I have only one wish in this world; to love him and him alone. For the rest he has carte blanche to do as he pleases in my regard. I just leave myself in his loving hands, and so have no anxiety or care, but great peace of soul.

Worries? Of course; and thank God. How else are you going to be a saint?

If you train yourself to see God's hand in all things and rather to be glad when everything goes wrong, you will enjoy great interior peace. Here is a most important spiritual maxim for you: A soul which is not at peace and happy will never be really holy.

You are not trusting him enough. Do stop worrying and leave this whole matter in his hands. This is only a trick of the devil to disturb your peace of soul; and without peace there can be no prayer, no union with God.

God wants to have your soul in a state of perfect peace and calm, for only then will he be able to fill it with his love and dwell there undisturbed.

Avoid worry, anxiety, uneasiness about anything. 'The devil's boiling pot' expresses this state of mind; one trouble ended, another crops up to take its place; the soul never at rest; there is no peace, no calm, and also no real holiness.

Penance

As a rule do not make any penance a great burden – it is better to discontinue it if it becomes such – nor do anything excessive.

Is it not a mockery to call ourselves the spouses of a crucified love if our lives are not to some extent crucified also?

Devotion to the Sacred Heart cannot exist without self-denial.

The mortification good for you may be measured by your peace of mind. If you find your soul troubled by the penance you practise, or feel urged to practise, you should suspect the spirit that is leading you. Give all you can, but let it be the 'cheerful giver,' whom God loves. When the sacrifice is costing you too much and ruffles the spirit, go a little slower and all will be well.

Every little victory in the matter of food is a real triumph, for this is a real test of generosity. Saint Francis de Sales used to say, 'Unless you deny your appetite, you will never be a saint' – a mighty saying!

Perfection
Perfection is loving more surely and entirely God's will and seeking it in his way and because it is his will.

Prayer
As regards prayer, you should try to follow the attraction of the Holy Spirit, for all souls are not led by the same path.

One word about the difficulty at prayer. It is an unnatural thing, that is a supernatural thing, and hence must always be hard; for prayer takes us out of our natural element. But pray on all the same.

There is no happiness to be compared to the sweets one tastes at times in prayer.

I think our Lord wants your whole day to be one continued act of love and union with him in your heart, which has no need of words to express it. Your attitude ought to be that of the mother beside the cot of her babe, lost in love and tenderness, but saying nothing, just letting the heart speak, though the wee one cannot know it as Jesus does. There is nothing more sanctifying than this life, which few, I fear, reach to, since it means a constant effort to bring back our wandering imagination.

By all means follow the guidance of the Holy Spirit and do not bind yourself to anything which you find a hindrance. Just let yourself 'sink into God' when in his presence. Don't try to pray in words, but love him which, of course, is the highest prayer and then abandon yourself to his pleasure, whether that be consolation or darkness.

We must be intellectually pious, that is, our piety should rest on the bedrock of principle, and not on mood, on sentiment, on spiritual consolation.

I assert fearlessly that if only we all prayed enough and I mean by that a constant, steady, unflagging stream of aspirations, petitions, etc., from the heart there is not one, no matter how imperfect, careless or even sinful, who would not become a saint and a big one.

Do not give up prayer on any account, no matter how dry or rotten you feel; every moment, especially before him in the tabernacle, is a certain, positive gain; the effect will be there though you may not feel it.

I think the best of all prayers is just to kneel quietly and let Jesus pour himself into your soul.

You ask how to pray well. The answer is, pray often, in season and out of season, against yourself, in spite of yourself. There is no other way.

Did it ever strike you that when our Lord pointed out the 'fields white for the harvest,' he did not urge his Apostle to go and reap it, but to pray?

'He went out into a mountain to pray; and he passed the whole night in the prayer of God.' (Luke 6:12). Christ prays, on his knees, humbly, reverently. I watch him well during this great act of his life. Lord, teach me how to pray like you. He goes up into a mountain, away from all that may distract him. He leaves his preaching, his work, even the thought of it, behind. In quiet and solitude. He goes on his knees, humbly as a creature, reverently as a child. He had gone through a long hard day's work, he was weary, longing for rest and sleep. Yet he passed the whole night in the prayer of God.

Presence of God

'No evil shall come upon you.' (Jeremiah. 23:17). It is a consoling thought that God watches over us with unceasing care; that no matter where we may be – alone in our humble cell or passing through the crowded streets of the feverish panting city – the hand of God is over us and sheltering us from a thousand unknown dangers, guiding us safely along the path of life. Wicked men may plot evil things against us, all the hellish horde may rage in fury round us, but harm us they cannot without his consent who directs all things for his own wise ends.

Present moment

Making my meditation before the picture of the *Curé of Ars*, he seemed to say to me with an interior voice: 'The secret of my life was that I lived for the moment. I did not say, "I must pray here for the next hour", but only "for this moment". I did not say, "I have a hundred confessions to hear", but looked upon this one as the first and last. I did not say, "I must deny myself everything and always", but only "just this once". By this means I was able always to do everything perfectly, quietly and in great peace. Try and live this life of the present moment. Pray as if you had nothing else whatever to do; say your Office slowly as if for the last time; do not look forward and think you must often repeat this act of self-denial. This will make all things much easier. No sacrifice would be great if looked at in this way. I do not feel now the pain which has past, I have not yet to bear what is coming; hence I have only to endure the suffering of this one moment, which is quickly over and cannot return.

Progress

It is useful from time to time to pause and ask ourselves if we are, like the child Jesus, growing in wisdom and grace. Does each evening see us farther on the path of perfection, more pleasing and dearer to God? When we lie down to rest, is it with the feeling that the day just passed has been one of progress in the spiritual life, of merit and victory over self?

Depend more on God. *You* cannot become holy, *you* cannot overcome your faults; but Jesus can give you help, strength and courage.

Sacrifice

I feel that I could go through fire and water to serve such a man as Napoleon, that no sacrifice he could ask would be too hard. What would the army think of me if Napoleon said, 'I want you to do so and so,' and I replied, 'But, your Majesty, I am very sensitive to cold, I want to have a sleep in the afternoon, to rest when I am tired, and I really could not do without plenty of good things to eat!' Would I not deserve to have my uniform torn from me and be driven from the army, not even allowed to serve in the ranks? How do I serve Jesus my King? What kind of service? Generous or making conditions? In easy things but not in hard ones? What have I done for Jesus? What am I doing for Jesus? What shall I do for Jesus?

'If any man will come after me, let him deny himself and take up his cross, and follow me.' (Matthew 16:24) With St Peter we tell our Lord that we will follow him; and the first time an occasion of going against ourselves turns up, we turn our back upon him: This saying is hard, can't do it. And yet this conquest of self is the following of Christ.

Saints

The heroism of the saints

Heroism is a virtue which has an attraction for every heart. It seems to lift us out of our petty selves and make us for a moment forget our own selfish interests. It appeals irresistibly to the noble-minded; even to the cowardly it is a powerful stimulus. Thus, it is that in all times the saints have ever had such an attraction for men – they are heroes!

Jesuit saints

The thought of our saints now in heaven should serve as a great encouragement to us to walk bravely in the way of holiness. On earth they led the life that we lead; there was little to distinguish them from the other members with whom they lived. Yet before

God what a vast difference! How perfectly each action was performed; with how much fervour, with what exact attention to each detail, with what intense love of God! Each moment brought its duty, each hour its allotted task; and all, both sweet and bitter, were joyfully accepted as the manifestation of the divine will in their regard. Thus the years sped swiftly by, leaving behind the sweet odour of a well-spent life.

St Joseph

I contrast the obedience of St Joseph with my obedience. His so prompt, unquestioning, uncomplaining, perfect; mine given so grudgingly; perhaps exterior without interior conformity.

St Mary Magdalen

Mary, penitent as she is, could not fully know the depth of her guilt, she had forgotten many sins; but Jesus saw all … In those few moments Mary had learnt a precious lesson: that peace, contentment, holiness are to be found at the feet of Jesus and there alone, that the delights of contemplation far outweighs the empty joys which the world offers.

St Peter

Saint Peter relied too much on himself; it was always 'I will do this' and 'I will do that'. If he had said: 'Lord, I know my own weakness, but I'll do it with Your help' it would have been quite different.

St Peter Claver[22]

Saint Peter Claver was one of those generous heroic souls whom God sends upon this earth to serve as a stimulus to our zeal, to urge us on to dare and do great things for his glory ... He saw these poor wretches dazed with their long confinement, sick in body and weary of soul, cast on the burning sand, their eyes wild with terror at the vision of the nameless death they thought awaited them. Here was scope for his zeal. Was not the image of Jesus stamped deep upon the souls of each of them? Did they not bear the likeness of the sacred humanity in their tortured limbs?

St Teresa of Ávila[23]

The life of St Teresa teaches us that we should never despair of becoming saints. As a child she was filled with a strange mysterious longing for martyrdom. But the early years of her religious life found her cold

---

22. Born in Spain in 1580 and died in Colombia in 1654. Peter Claver entered the Jesuits at the age of twenty, and while a student in Mallorca he came under the influence of fellow Jesuit St Alphonsus Rodriguez. Peter Claver was renowned for his care for slaves who were being shipped from Africa to Colombia. He encountered unimaginable suffering when entering the slave ships and provided material and spiritual support for an estimated three hundred thousand slaves.

23. Born in 1515 and died in 1582, Teresa of Ávila was a Spanish Carmelite and mystic who reformed the Carmelite order of her time. She is renowned for her spiritual writings and is a Doctor of the Church.

or tepid in the service of God, indifferent to the sacred duties of her state. The call came. Sweetly in her ear sounded that little voice which too often in other souls has been hushed and stifled. Teresa rose. The past was gone and no lamenting could recall its ill-spent days, but the present was hers, and the future lay before her. Ungenerous in the past, generosity would be her darling virtue; cold and careless, no one would now equal her burning love for her saviour.

Saint Francis Xavier[24]

Xavier's hour has come, the hour of his eternal reward and never-ending bliss. In a little hut, open on all sides to the biting blast, the great apostle lies dying. Far from home and all that makes this life pleasant, far from the quiet of his own religious house, alone upon this barren isle, our saint will yield his soul to God. What joy fills his heart now at the thought of the sacrifices he has made, the honours he has despised, the pleasures left behind. Happy sufferings! Happy penances! He thinks of what his life might have been, the life of a gay worldling, and in gratitude he lifts his

24. Born in 1506 in Spain and died in 1552 off the coast of China. Francis Xavier was one of the first Jesuits, recruited by Ignatius of Loyola at the University of Paris. He was a zealous missionary who travelled throughout Asia. His great dream was to evangelise China, but he died on an island off the coast of China, worn out from his labours aged only forty-six. He is the patron saint of missionaries.

eyes to thank his God for the graces given him. What matter now the hardships he has endured? All, all, are past, for now the sweet reward of heaven is inviting him to his eternal rest.

St Benedict Joseph Labre[25]

During the journey I felt our Lord wanted to give me some message through St Benedict Joseph Labre. No light came while praying in the Church or in the house; but when I went up to his little room and knelt down a voice seemed to whisper 'Read what is written on the wall'. I saw these words "God calls me to an austere life; I must prepare myself to follow the ways of God". With these words came a sudden light to see how much one gains by every act of sacrifice.

St Therese[26]

I wish I could tell you of the peace and strength one feels praying at the grave of the 'Little Flower', and

25. Born in Amettes, France in 1748 and died in Rome in 1783. Benedict Joseph Labre tried unsuccessfully to enter several monasteries. He became a wandering pilgrim, visiting holy shrines and living on the streets of Rome. Even as a homeless beggar he was renowned for his holiness, and when he died the children of Rome ran through the streets proclaiming that the saint was dead. Father Doyle seems to have had a fascination with this saint, even from his childhood, and mentions him several times in his diaries.

26. Born in 1873 and died in 1897 in France. Popularly known as the 'Little Flower', Therese Martin was born in the same year

I am hopeful that Soeur Therese will do as much for you as she has done for me.

Silence

Let us love silence and recollection. When we are at home with silence we are at home with God.

Silence seems impossible to busy people. But 'silence of the heart', interior silence, is always possible.

Spiritual doubt

You seemed to be troubled that you cannot love God when trials come and all is darkness. But that is just the moment when you love him most and prove your love the best. If only, when you are in desolation and dryness, you force yourself to utter an act of love or an oblation of yourself without a particle of feeling, you make an offering which is of surpassing value in his eyes and most pleasing to his Sacred Heart. A dry act of love is a real act of love, since it is all for Jesus and nothing for self. Therefore, welcome the hard black days as real harvest time.

Suffering

All my life my study has been to avoid suffering as

---

as Fr Doyle, and he had an attraction for her core message of spiritual childhood and faithfulness in little things. She is a Doctor of the Church.

much as possible, to make my life a comfortable one. How unlike my Jesus I have been, who sought to suffer on every occasion for me. I should be glad when pain comes and welcome it, because it makes me more like Jesus.

Try to take your days one by one as they come to you. The hard things of yesterday are past, and you are not asked to bear what tomorrow may have in store; so that the cross is really light when you take it bit by bit.

Talents

Look upon the grace God gives you as a talent you must work with and increase. The master in the Gospel gave his profitable servants twice as many talents. In like manner, will God double your grace if you make good use of it. He will give you 'grace for grace' (John 1:16).

Temptation

The net result of your temptations is a deeper humility, a sense of your own weakness and wretchedness, and is not this all gain?

There is a danger you may not suspect in thinking and grieving too much over temptation and faults. First of all there is oftentimes a secret pride hidden in our grief and anger with ourselves for not being as perfect as we thought, or as others thought. Then this worrying over what cannot well be avoided distracts the soul from God. After all, what God wants from you is love, and nothing should distract you from the grand work of love-giving. Hence when you fail, treat our Blessed Lord like a loving little child, tell him you are sorry, kiss his feet as a token of your regret, and then forget all about your naughtiness.

If you fight the temptations for a little while, great peace will soon come. Be brave and generous for the sake of our dear Lord, who loves you so much. If you have given in a little, don't lose a moment, but start away again.

You remember St Paul's bitter complaint that the good he wished to do he did not: 'I am delighted with the law of God, but I see another law in my members, fighting against the law of my mind and captivating me in the law of sin'. This is the experience of all who are striving to serve God well. They cannot always do what they would like and what they know he asks of them, but in the end the grace of God – St Paul's remedy – will bring the victory, if only we persevere.

The will

Without a big ardent desire, nothing will be done. 'If thou wilt be perfect,' our Lord once said, implying that sanctification is largely a question of good will. This, then, is the first grace you must pray for: the desire to be a saint.

A mother puts her little child on its feet, but the child itself must do something, must make an effort if it wants to walk. God does all that is necessary, but man must do his share.

It depends entirely on myself whether I become a saint or not. If I wish and will to be one, half the battle is over. Certainly God's help is secured. Every fresh effort to become holy gets fresh grace, and grace is what makes the soul holy and pleasing to God.

Why are we not saints? Want of courage and want of patience. We give up, we have not the strength of will and determination to succeed which the saints had.

Do I ever say, when an occasion of denying myself comes, 'It's too hard, I am no saint?' Might it not be asked of me in justice, 'Why aren't you? It is your business to be one, God intends you should be one, but you are too lazy, you won't take the trouble.'

We must not drag Christ down to our own level, but rather we must let Christ lift us up to his level.

Holiness and perfection depend on yourself, not on the actions of others.

A want of will is the chief obstacle to our becoming saints. We are not holy because we do not really wish to become so. We would indeed gladly possess the virtues of the saints: their humility and patience, their love of suffering, their penance and zeal. But we are unwilling to embrace all that goes to make a saint and to enter on the narrow path which leads to sanctity. A strong will, a resolute will, is needed; a will which is not to be broken by difficulties or turned aside by trifling obstacles; a determination to be a saint and not to faint and falter because the way seems long and hard and narrow. A big heart, a courageous heart, is needed for sanctification, to fight our worst enemy: our own self-love.

Trust in God

The priest turns and raises aloft the sacred host. In loving adoration, in reverent awe, the invisible angels fall prostrate. The bell tinkles softly, fragrant clouds of sweet-smelling incense ascend on high, and in the remotest corner of the vast church every head is bowed in adoration. It is a solemn moment, a moment when the silent streams of grace pour down upon our souls. God's hands are lifted up to bless us; his sacred face is turned upon us, and he waits so eagerly for us to ask some favour that he may win our hearts by his generosity. Let us ask, then, confidently and show our trust in God's great goodness by the boldness of our requests.

'Let him act,' must be your motto. Jesus will bring all things right in the end. The more I get to know God, the more inclined I feel to let him work out things in his own way and time, and to go on peacefully not troubling about anything.

Unity of life

How many wish to belong entirely to Jesus without reserve or restriction? Most want to serve two masters, to be under two standards. A union of worldliness and devotion; a perpetual succession of sins and repentance; something given to grace, more to nature; fervour and tepidity by turns … No service is so hard as the half-and-half; what is given to God costs more; his yoke is heavy; the cross is dragged, not cheerfully carried; the thought of what is refused to grace causes remorse and sadness; there is no pleasure from the world and little from the service of Christ.

Use of time

We should call a man a fool who wasted his wealth warming himself before a fire made of banknotes. Do we act less madly in seeking gratification by consuming our precious day in frivolities?

We love our life, cling to it, hug it, study how to prolong it, rebel if God thinks fit to shorten its span, nay, when we have run our scriptural appointed course 'three score and ten' (Psalm 90) we hunger for more.

But do we ever seriously ask ourselves, 'Does this life carry any responsibility with it?'

The soft chimes of the Angelus bell mark the fall of evening. Another day is gone. Another precious day, our measurement of God's most precious gift, time, has passed away and is swallowed up in the vast gulf of the irrevocable past. Another day has past! Another stage of our journey towards our final end is traversed. Nearer still than yesterday to that solemn moment of our lives, its end; nearer still to heaven with its joys unknown, untasted; nearer still to him for whom we labour now and strive to serve. How many more days are left? Too few alas! for all we have to do, but not so few that we cannot heap them high with noble deeds and victories bravely won.

Life is only a day quickly passed and gone, but the merit of it, the glory given to God, will remain for ever. Give him all you can generously and lovingly, do not let one little sacrifice escape you, they are dear to him because he finds so few really generous souls who think only of him and never of themselves.

I can imagine I am a soul in hell, and God in his mercy is saying to me, 'Return to the world for this year and on your manner of life during the year will depend your returning to hell or not'. What a life I should lead! How little I should think of suffering, of mortification! How I would rejoice in suffering! How perfectly each moment would be spent!

God has many gifts to bestow upon us, but none more precious than time. Yet how we abuse this royal gift! How little we think of it! How we despise these golden moments, moments whose true value we shall not really prize till alas! too late when time shall be no more for us.

Work

Work for Jesus! Yes, though the weary head may ache and the tired brain refuse to act. Work on, work on; the years slip by and soon the hour of toil will cease for ever. Work for Jesus! How sweet these words! Not one effort escapes his watchful eye and he will reward you with a joy unknown for what you suffer now.

Women

All through his life of hardship and persecution, women were faithful to him [Jesus] and showed him reverence. A woman's voice from the crowd had been raised to bless him as he preached. Women ministered to his wants, received him into their houses when all other doors were closed against him, lavished on him costly gifts which even his disciples grudged him. In his hour of need a woman's voice alone was raised in his defence and heedless of the rough soldiers and the hooting rabble, a crowd of women pressed around him and filled the air with their lamentation.

Chapter Four:
Priesthood and Vocations

One of Fr Doyle's most enduring but hidden legacies was his work in fostering vocations. He helped many young women find suitable convents at the time when convents in Ireland were full to capacity, and he assisted young men with their seminary education through innovative fundraising schemes. He wrote two bestselling booklets on these themes.

This chapter includes an excerpt from a letter on this theme written three weeks before his death, as well as selected extracts from his vocational pamphlets.

Fr Doyle's work for vocations
Letter to his father, 25 July 1917
You will be glad to know, as I was, that the ninth edition (ninety thousand copies) of my little book, *Vocations*, is rapidly being exhausted. After my ordination, when I began to be consulted on this important subject, I was struck by the fact that there was nothing one could put into the hands of boys and girls to help them to a decision, except ponderous volumes, which they would scarcely read … I realised the want for some time; but one evening as I walked back to the train after dining with you, the thought

of the absolute necessity for such a book seized me so strongly, that there and then I made up my mind to persuade someone to write it, for I never dreamt of even attempting the task myself.

I soon found out that the shortest way to get a thing done is to do it yourself ... I remember well when the manuscript had passed the censors to my great surprise, the venerable manager of the Messenger Office began shaking his head over the prospect of its selling, for as he said with truth, 'It is a subject which appeals to a limited few'. He decided to print five thousand, and hinted I might buy them all myself!

Then when the pamphlet began to sell and orders to come in fast, I began to entertain the wild hope that by the time I reached the stage of two crutches and a long white beard, I might possibly see the one hundred thousand mark reached. We are nearly at that now without any pushing or advertising, and I hope the crutches and flowing beard are still a long way off. God is good, is he not? As the second edition came out only in the beginning of 1914 the sale has been extraordinarily rapid.

It is consoling from time to time to receive letters from convents or religious houses, saying that some novice had come to them chiefly through reading *Vocations*; for undoubtedly there are many splendid soldiers lost to Christ's army for the want of a little help and encouragement.

Excerpts from *Vocations*

First published in August 1915, several hundred thousand copies of the pamphlet were sold in eight different languages

'Good Master, what good shall I do that I may have life everlasting?' It was the eager question of one whom fortune had blessed with the wealth of this world, but who realised that life eternal was a far more precious treasure. He had come to the divine teacher, seeking what he must yet do to make secure the great prize for which he was striving. He was young and wealthy, a ruler in the land, one whose life had been without stain or blemish.

'The Commandments? – All these have I kept from my youth,' he had said; 'Good Master, what is yet wanting to me?' Jesus looked on him with love, for such a soul was dear to his Sacred Heart. 'If thou wilt be perfect,' comes the answer, 'go sell what thou hast and give to the poor, and come, follow me.'

There was a painful pause: nature and grace were struggling for the mastery; the invitation had been given, the road to perfection pointed out. There was only one sacrifice needed to make him a true disciple, but it was a big one, too great for him who lately seemed so generous. He hesitates, wavers, and then sadly turns away, with the words 'Come, follow Me,' ringing in his ears, for love of his great possessions had wrapped itself round his heart – a vocation had been offered and refused …

Nearly two thousand years have passed since then, but unceasingly that same voice has been whispering in the ears of many a lad and maiden, 'One thing is yet wanting to you – come, follow me'. Some have heard that voice with joy and gladness of heart, and have risen up at the master's call; others have stopped their ears, or turned away in fear from the side of him who beckoned to them, while not a few have stood and listened, wondering what it meant, asking themselves could such an invitation be for them, till Jesus of Nazareth passed by and they were left behind forever. To these, chiefly, is this simple explanation of a vocation offered, in the hope that they may recognise the workings of grace within their souls, or be moved to beg that they may one day be sharers in this crowning gift of God's eternal love …

Long ago, while yet the Saviour trod this earth, we read that once he sat by the well-side, weary from his journeyings. As he paused to rest, his gaze fell upon the waving cornfields stretching far out of sight, the ears bending under their load of countless, tiny seeds, each bearing its germ of life. To the eyes of his soul, devoured with a burning zeal, it was an image of the vast multitude of human beings he had come to save, of the souls of those with whom he lived and the myriads who would follow him. Silently he looks at the solitary husbandman, sickle in hand, slowly gathering the sheaves of golden corn, then sadly turning to the disciples, he says, with a hidden meaning in his words:

'The harvest indeed is great, but the labourers are few. Pray ye, therefore, the Lord of the harvest that he send labourers into his harvest.'

The words died away, but their echo has never ceased to sound. 'The harvest is great, but the labourers are few.' Turn where we will, in no matter what part of the globe, and there we shall see still the harvest of souls, waiting to be garnered into the master's granaries …

Boys and girls of Ireland, with your young lives so full of promise opening out before you, have you no nobler ideals, no loftier ambition, than to spend your days in pleasure and amusement, while your brothers and your sisters look appealingly to you for help? Lift up your eyes and see the harvest awaiting you, the most glorious work ever given man to do – the saving of immortal souls. The day of Ireland's greatest glory was the time when the land was covered with a golden network of schools and monasteries; when her missioners and nuns were to be found in every clime and country; when every tenth Irishman and woman was consecrated to God and His service … This is the work that lies before you, the work God looks to you to do – strengthening the faith that St Patrick left us, preaching the truth to an unbelieving world, sacrificing yourselves, as your ancestors did before you, leaving home and friends, and, for the sake of God and Ireland, giving your life that others may be saved.

A vocation is, indeed, the gift of God, but through love for the souls whom he longs to save, gladly would he bestow it on many more, if only they would listen to his voice or ask him for this treasure.

Excerpts from *Shall I be a Priest?*

First published in 1915 and translated into nine languages

We turn our thoughts back to the days of Our Lord, to the time when the meek saviour lived amongst men. Darkness has stretched her mantle over the land, bringing repose and sleep to every living thing, but out on the lonely mountain top a solitary figure kneels in prayer. With bowed head and uplifted hands the divine redeemer pours out the 'Prayer of God' that his heavenly father's blessing may come down upon the work he is about to do.

'And when day was come, he called unto him his disciples, and he chose twelve of them whom he also named Apostles' (Luke 6). Lovingly the saviour must have looked upon the little band, for they were to be his priests, the first ministers of the new law he had come from heaven to establish. They were only poor, rough fishermen, but strong with the divine commission to 'teach and baptise.' Each of the twelve would carry their master's name to the ends of the earth. To them he would give the power not possessed by the mighty angels, the power 'to bind and loose,' and change the bread and wine into his own body and blood.

'You have not chosen me,' he said, as he saw the shrinking humility of his astonished followers, 'You have not chosen me, but I have chosen you' for an honour and dignity unknown in the world before. 'I will not now call you servants, but I have called you friends, because all things whatsoever I have heard of my father, I have made known to you.'

'You are the salt of the earth' to season men's lives with the savour of holiness; 'You are the light of the world' to lead every straying soul to me. Deeply conscious of his own great unworthiness, his faults and failings, many and great though they be, the priest can never forget the loftiness of his calling and that he is the elect of God ...

The Ambassador of Christ! A glorious title for anyone to claim! As Ambassador, sent by the king of heaven and earth to bring his message of 'peace and good will' to all men; a liberator, with power to break the chains of hell and set free the souls held captive by the fetters of sin; a consoler, bearing the balm of consolation to bleeding hearts, bringing back lost happiness by the certainty of forgiveness; the representative of God himself, raised up to continue his own work: 'All power is given to me in heaven and on earth, go ye, therefore, and teach all nations; whosoever heareth you heareth me; behold I am with you all days even to the consummation of the world ...'

How little the world thinks of the priest of God! How little it realises all it owes to him; the chastisement for sin he has warded off, the graces he has won for others, the help he has been to weary hearts, the souls he has saved from hell. He goes on his way, at times despised and hated, his faults and failings magnified, as if he were not still a man, but the power of God goes with him, the grace of God surrounds him, while love, respect, and reverence follow his footsteps from those who know all they owe to the humble priest, the Ambassador of Christ on earth …

Unfortunately, some parents look upon a vocation in the family as a sort of social catastrophe. They may not, perhaps, go so far as directly to crush out the desire for a higher life, which God has planted in their child's heart, but they give it no encouragement. They speak of the advantages of the various professions, the fame to be won as a lawyer or doctor, the glory of a military career, the triumphs of the diplomatic service, forgetting the saying of St Vincent de Paul, 'There is no grander work on earth than to form a priest,' no calling nobler or more honourable than to labour for the salvation of souls as the Ambassador of Christ. No wonder the hearts of so few young men are fired by this noblest form of ambition, the longing to serve the King of kings, or aspire to the unspeakable dignity of the priesthood …

Chapter Five:
Meditations on the
Stations of the Cross

The Stations of the Cross are a traditional Catholic devotion during which the faithful meditate on key scenes from Christ's passion. Father Doyle's text, written in his personal diaries in January 1906, is typical of his own spirit and of the era in which he lived. His aim is to foster repentance for our sins, compassion for Christ in his sufferings, and encourage more generous service of Christ.

The First Station: Jesus is condemned to death

Around the judgement seat are grouped a motley crowd. Men and women of every rank, the high-born Jewish maiden, the rough Samaritan woman; haughty Scribes and proud Pharisees mingle with the common loafer of the great city. Hatred has united them all for one common object; hatred of one who ever loves them and to their wild fury has only opposed acts of gentle kindness. A mighty scream goes up, a scream of fierce rage and angry fury, such a sound as only could be drawn from the very depths of hell. 'Death to him! Death to the false prophet!' He has spent his life among you doing good – Let him die! He has healed your sick, given strength to the palsied, sight to your blind – Let him die! He has raised your dead – Let death be his fate!

The Second Station: Jesus takes up his cross

Away from the palace now a sad procession is winding. On the faces of the multitude a fiendish joy is written, they have had their wish and now issue forth to glut their eyes on the dying struggles of the suffering innocent one. Painfully he is toiling up the long narrow street, narrower still from the crowds that line the way; each step is agony, each yard of ground he covers a fresh martyrdom of ever increasing suffering. With a refinement of cruelty his enemies have placed upon his shoulders the heavy, rough beams which will be his last painful resting place. Cruelly the heavy beam weighs upon his mangled flesh and cuts and chafes a long, raw sore deep to the very bone.

The Third Station: Jesus falls for the first time

Bravely has our Lord borne the galling weight of his cross; bravely has he struggled on, tottering and stumbling, longing for a moment's rest, yearning for a respite however short. But rest he will not, that he may teach us how unfalteringly we must press on to our goal. But nature will have its way. His sight grows dim; his strength fails and with a crash our Saviour lies extended on the ground. Oh! if you have not hearts of stone let him lie even thus, poor, crushed and broken thing. If you have but one spark of compassion left, one tender feeling of sympathy urge him not on awhile, so spent, so weary. On a poor maimed brute you have pity – think of the sorrow of him extended there.

The Fourth Station: Jesus meets his Blessed Mother

To sensitive souls the pain they cause others is far worse than any sufferings they may endure themselves. They may have much to endure, but to see others in pain causes them deeper grief. Jesus and Mary meet. Alone he could have suffered with joy so that she, his dearest mother, might have been spared the agony of seeing all he must endure. With one look of pity Jesus reads the anguish of that cruelly lacerated heart; with one long gaze of infinite love and pity Mary sees the depth of her son's woe, his long hours of torture, his utter weariness, his sorrow, his grief, his anguish. May she not help him? At least lift for one moment that cross?

The Fifth Station: St Simon of Cyrene helps Jesus to carry His cross

When God lays a cross upon us, some misfortune, some unexpected burden, instead of thanking him for this precious gift, too often we rebel against his will. We forget that our Saviour never sends a cross alone, but ever sweetens its bitterness, lightens its weight by his all-powerful grace. With reluctance, with unwillingness, Simon bears the cross of his master. At first his spirit revolted against this injustice, his pride rebelled against this ignominy. But once he accepted with resignation, his soul was filled with heavenly sweetness, he felt not the weight of the heavy beams, he heeded not the jibes of the multitude but pressed on after his master, proud to be his follower.

The Sixth Station: Veronica wipes the face of Jesus

As the sorrowful procession moves slowly on, a woman, who with anxious gaze has watched its approach, steps forward and wipes the sacred face of Jesus. It is a simple action, yet reveals the kindly thoughtfulness of a charitable heart. Gladly would Veronica have done all in her power to lessen the sufferings of the Lord, to ease the dreadful burden which was crushing him, to show some mark of sympathy and compassion. That little act of love touched the broken heart of Jesus; she wipes the clotted blood and streaming sweat from his face, leaving his sacred image stamped on the veil of Veronica; but deeper and more clear cut did he impress on her heart the memory of his passion.

The Seventh Station: Jesus falls the second time

Jesus falls a second time, crushed beneath the weight of his awful sufferings which are fast draining his strength. Exhausted and spent he lies upon the rough-paved ground, a cruel resting place for his bleeding, lacerated body. Vainly he tries to rise, for love impels him on to the consummation of the sacrifice, but his tottering limbs will not support him and once again he falls upon the ground. Again, the soldiers with fiendish brutality drag him to his feet with coarse jibes and mocking laughter, with kicks and blows they drive him on, pulling him now forward, now back, striving if possible to add to the sufferings of the patient victim.

The Eighth Station: Jesus consoles the women of Jerusalem

The disciples of Jesus have deserted their master, and fearful for their own safety, have abandoned him to his fate. Peter who would die for him, Matthew who left all to follow him; both are far from him now and dread to be pointed to as his friends. Yet Jesus is not alone. A few, a faithful few, remain beside him still, poor, weak women, but strong with the courage of love. The brutal crowd surge round, inflamed with hate and lust for blood; but they offer him the tribute of a woman's heart – the silent tears of sympathy. 'Weep not for me,' he says, 'weep rather for those who unlike these my executioners will one day crucify me again with full knowledge of what they do.'

The Ninth Station: Jesus falls the third time

The hill of Calvary is almost reached, the hour of the great sacrifice is at hand. Still the heart of Jesus thirsts for suffering to show his great, his all devouring love for us. Again he falls! With limbs, all bruised and broken, with a body all one raw, red, quivering sore, each step he took was agony. But to fall thus helpless on the ragged ground, to be kicked and beaten as he lay with nerveless limbs all paralysed with pain must have been to his high-strung, delicate frame a thousand-fold martyrdom. The executioners were alarmed. Was death going to rob them of their victim and cheat them of the joy they promised themselves as their victim writhed in the agonies of death?

The Tenth Station: Jesus is stripped of his garments

At last he stands upon the hill of shame to pay the price of our redemption. In the eyes of his eternal father, a sinner laden with the crimes of a wicked world; before men, the most abject and abandoned of creatures. A brutal soldier advances. He lays his hand upon the garment of Jesus and roughly tears it from his sacred shoulders. The cloth has sunk deeply into the gaping wounds left by the recent scourging, and driven deeper still by the weight of the cross and the oft-repeated blows. With a horrid, rending sound the wounds are torn open afresh, the sacred blood gushes forth anew and bathes his limbs in its ruddy stream. It is a moment of awful agony.

The Eleventh Station: Jesus is nailed to the cross

Upon his last resting place Jesus lays himself down. No soft bed, no easy couch to ease the agony of his aching limbs, but a hard, rough beam must be his place of death. Meekly he extends his arms, those arms ever open to welcome back the repentant sinner, and offers his hands to be pierced as the prophet had foretold. A long, blunt nail is placed upon the palm: a heavy, dull thud, the crunch of parting flesh and rending muscle, the spouting crimson blood which covers the face and hands of the hardened soldier and Jesus is fastened to the cross. Come, sinner, gaze upon your work for you have nailed him there! Your sins it was which flung your saviour down, your sins which drove the iron deep into his sacred flesh.

The Twelfth Station: Jesus dies on the cross

Upon the cross he hangs now, the most abject and despised of all men, the butt for vile jests, a common mark for all to hurl their jibes at. There he hangs, in agony no human lips can tell, no mind conceives, an impostor, a vile hypocrite, a failure. 'He came to make himself a king! See, we have crowned his brow with a royal, sparkling diadem. He sought a kingdom! From that elevated throne let him look upon the land which will never be his now. He threatened our scribes with woes and punishments, let him look to his own fate and if he has that power which some say was his, let him come down now from the cross and we too shall believe in his word.'

The Thirteenth Station: Jesus is taken down from the cross

Mary stands at the foot of the cross to receive in her arms the lifeless body of her son. Once more his head is resting on her bosom as it used to do long years ago when a little child he nestled to his mother's breast. But now that sacred head is bruised and swollen, stamped with the cruel mark of the mocking diadem; His hair all clotted with the oozing blood, tangled and in disorder. Even she, upon whose heart is stamped every lineament of her son's dear face, can scarcely recognise his features now. On every line is marked the anguish of long-drawn agony, of torture and agonising pain, of woe, unutterable woe, of sorrow, suffering and abandonment.

The Fourteenth Station: Jesus is laid in the tomb

The final scene of the awful tragedy is drawing to a close. Reverently the faithful few bear the dead Christ down the hill of shame, that body from which all the care of loving hands cannot remove the marks of the cruel scourge, the rending nails, the lance's gaping thrust. Into the tomb they bear him, the burial place of a stranger, best suited to him who during his life had not where to lay his head. Reverently they lay him down; one last, fond embrace of his own mother before they lead her hence, and then in silence and in sorrow they leave him, their dearest master, to the watchful care of God's own angels. Sin has done its work! Sin has triumphed, but its very triumph will prove its own undoing.

Chapter Six:
Personal Prayers

The prayers in this chapter appear in various letters or diary entries written by Fr Doyle and were mostly intended for his own private use. It ends with the text of a meditation on a scene from the Gospel of Mathew that Fr Doyle used in his retreats.

Prayer of abandonment

Take, O Lord, and receive my liberty, my health and strength, my limbs, my flesh, my blood, my very life. Do with me just as you wish; I embrace all lovingly – sufferings, wounds, death – if only it will glorify you one tiny bit.

Passion of Christ, comfort me!

Passion of Christ, comfort me! Comfort me, for the day is long and weary; comfort me as I fight my way up the path of life safe to the haven of thy Sacred Heart, comfort me in sorrow, in pain, in sickness. Comfort me when temptation rages round me and every hope seems lost, and when that last dread hour has sounded and my eyes are closing on this world of sin, oh, passion of Christ! comfort me then, and lead me gently to thy wounded sacred feet above.

Prayer of trust in a time of trial

God sometimes seems to ask the impossible, a sorrow, a cross. Oh! it would crush me! How can this be? How? Lord, I do not know how, but you do. I will trust you always.

Lord, that I may see

Jesus is looking at me as once he did upon blind Bartimeus. 'What wilt thou that I do to thee?' (Luke 18, 41). Lord, that I may see myself as you see me. Lord, that my eyes may be open to the shortness of life. Lord, that I may understand the value of one degree of merit, and so heap up many.

Prayer to the Holy Spirit

Come, O Holy Ghost, into my heart and make me holy so that I may be generous with God and become a saint.

The burning love of Jesus

O Jesus, Jesus, Jesus! who would not love you, who would not give their heart's blood for you, if only once they realised the depth and the breadth and the realness of your burning love? Why not then make every human heart a burning furnace of love for you, so that sin would become an impossibility, sacrifice a pleasure and a joy, virtue the longing of every soul, so that we should live for love, dream of love, breathe your love, and at last die of a broken heart of love, pierced through and through with the shaft of love, the sweetest gift of God to man.

I will serve you till death

Lord, you know I love you less than any other, but I long and desire to love you more than all the rest. Take my heart, dear Lord, and hide it in your own, that so I may only love what you love and desire what you desire. May I find no pleasure in the things of this world, its pleasures and amusement; but may my one delight be in thinking of you, working for you, loving you, and staying in your sweet presence before the tabernacle. Why do you want my love, dear Jesus, and why have you left me no rest all these years till I gave you at last my poor heart to love you, and you alone? This ceaseless pleading for my love fills me with hope and confidence that, sinful as my life has been in the past, you have forgiven and forgotten it all. Thanks a million times, dearest Jesus, for all your goodness. I will love and serve you now till death.

To stamp out sin

My God, give me an intense hatred and dread and horror of the smallest sin. I want to please you and love you and serve you as I have never done before. Let me begin by stamping out all sin in my soul.

Lord, I cannot resist you

O my God, I feel now as if I cannot resist you longer. Your infinite patience and desire to bring me to you has broken the ice of my cold heart. I will arise and go to you, humbled and sorrowful, and for the rest of my life give you of my very best. Help me, sweet Jesus, by your grace, for I am weak and cowardly.

Jesus I want to please you

Jesus, dear Jesus, I want to please you, to do exactly what you want of me, to give all generously this time without any reserve, and never to go back on my resolution.

Prayer for generosity

I want to be generous with God and to refuse him nothing. I do not want to say, 'I will go just so far and no farther'. My loving Jesus, I will, I will be generous with you now at last. But you must aid me, it must be your work, I am so cowardly. Make me see clearly your holy will.

Prayer in time of trial

Oh, Master! I come to your feet to tell you all. I have buried my dead. I have lost what can never be restored to me in this world. I have come from the grave with half myself buried there. I have come back to a life with all its meaning gone from it – a life without joy, interest, anything to which my soul responds – a dreary waste stretching before and that I must cross alone. Where shall I turn for courage and for strength? Where but to you, to whom the disciples of John turned in their desolation? Open to me your arms and your heart. Listen to me tenderly whilst I tell you all my trouble. Speak to my soul and calm and strengthen it. Make up to me for what you have taken away. And if you ask me what compensation I desire, I answer: 'None other than thyself, O Lord.'

Prayer for priests

O my God, pour out in abundance thy spirit of sacrifice upon thy priests. It is both their glory and their duty to become victims, to be burnt up for souls, to live without ordinary joys, to be often the objects of distrust, injustice and persecution. The words they say every day at the altar, 'This is my body, this is my blood,' grant them to apply to themselves: 'I am no longer myself, I am Jesus, Jesus crucified. I am, like the bread and wine, a substance no longer itself, but by consecration another.'

O my God, I burn with desire for the sanctification of thy priests. I wish all the priestly hands which touch thee were hands whose touch is gentle and pleasing to thee, that all the mouths uttering such sublime words at the altar should never descend to speaking trivialities.

Let priests in all their person stay at the level of their lofty functions, let every man find them simple and great, like the Holy Eucharist, accessible to all yet above the rest of men. O my God, grant them to carry with them from the Mass of today, a thirst for the Mass of tomorrow, and grant them, ladened themselves with gifts, to share these abundantly with their fellow men. Amen.

Some aspirations of Fr Doyle

My Crucified Jesus, help me to crucify myself.

Lord, teach me how to pray and pray always.

Jesus, thou saint of saints, make me a saint.

Blessed be God for all things.

My loving Jesus within my heart unite my heart to thee.

Heart of Jesus, give me your zeal for souls.

My God, thou art omnipotent, make me a saint.

My Jesus, help me now to work for you, to slave for you, to fight for you, and then to die for you!

O Jesus, I am so weak, help me to give you all and to do it now.

Gospel meditation: Matthew 14:22-36[27]

'About the fourth watch of the night he cometh to them'

Christ did not show Himself until the fourth watch of the night. How often is this same history repeated in our own case! There is no encouragement, no comfort. We are wearied waiting. There is no sign

---

27. In this Gospel scene, the apostles spend a fearful night in a boat that is lashed by a storm. Jesus walks across the water to them in the fourth watch of the night, and bids Peter to walk to him across the water. Peter initially walks upon the water, but begins to doubt and then begins to sink.

of approaching help. Why not give up! Surely we never bargained for this. We never believed things would come to such a pass! Oh, the anguish of these moments, when in the midst of struggle, depression and loneliness Christ withholds his sensible presence.

Christ delays to come. But he is watching all the time; he would only test us. Let him not be disappointed. This is a moment of tremendous grace. If we are stout of heart and bear our trial manfully, we will emerge from the crucible with well-nigh herculean strength. These are moments that disentangle us from many of the trappings that weaken and weigh us down. After they have passed, invariably we find our vision clearer and our appreciation of the value of things truer.

Walking upon the sea
Thus does he come to us also walking upon the sea with these words upon his lips: 'Have a good heart, fear not, it is I.' And we whisper to ourselves, 'It is the Lord.' Yes, then we understand. Then everything goes easy and we wonder that we should ever have doubted. Then we are ashamed of our wavering. What a beautiful tribute to Christ our trust would have been. So we determine next time we will understand. We decide that when next the tide of our life runs high, when our heart-boat is lashed by a rugged sea, we will understand that Christ is near, watching us and we fight fearlessly and cheerfully. Thus, little by little, troubles and crosses will serve to clamp the trust in

Christ that will steady our hearts and like St Peter we too will cry out: 'Lord if it be thou, bid me to come to thee across the waters.' O the joy of our hearts as the master says 'Come.' And we go. We really walk upon the sea. We do wonders until some tremendous sorrow-wave dashes up between us and Christ, and for a moment we lose heart and cry out 'Lord save me'.

Immediately he spoke with them
Immediately – that word is full of love – stretching forth his hand he takes hold of me. And when He has come into my heart-boat the wind ceased. But it is only after Christ has been given full control of our heart-boat that the winds cease. This is the struggle of our life – *to let Christ rule.*

So long as he must come over the waters to us there will be many a lonely struggle. But when through great generosity on our part we have emptied our lives of everything likely to raise a tempest in the heart, then Christ will sit at the helm and the waves may toss, the winds may roll and blow about the boat. We are calm. We have no cause to fear. Christ sits at the helm and rules.

Appendix:
Testimonies

Major General Sir William Bernard Hickie[28]

Father Doyle was one of the best priests I have ever met, and one of the bravest men who have fought or worked out here. He did his duty, and more than his duty, most nobly, and has left a memory and a name behind him that will never be forgotten. On the day of his death, 16 August, he had worked in the front line, and even in front of that line, and appeared to know no fatigue – he never knew fear. He was killed by a shell towards the close of the day, and was buried on the Frezenberg Ridge … He was recommended for the Victoria Cross by his commanding officer, by his brigadier, and by myself. Superior authority, however, has not granted it, and as no other posthumous reward is given, his name will, I believe, be mentioned in the

---

28. Major General Hickie (1865-1950) was Commander of the 16th (Irish) Division. The above quote is taken from a letter he wrote to a friend. Writing some months later to Mr Hugh Doyle, he said: 'I could not say too much about your son. He was loved and reverenced by us all; his gallantry, self-sacrifice, and devotion to duty were all so well-known and recognised. I think that his was the most wonderful character that I have ever known.'

commander-in-chief's despatch…I can say without boasting that this is a division of brave men; and even among these, Fr Doyle stood out.

Sergeant T. Flynn[29], *Irish News*, 29 August 1917

We had the misfortune to lose our chaplain, Fr Doyle, the other day. He was a real saint and would never leave his men, and it was really marvelous to see him burying dead soldiers under terrible shell fire. He did not know what fear was, and everybody in the battalion, Catholic and Protestant alike, idolised him. I went to Confession to him and received Holy Communion from him a day or two before he was killed, and I feel terribly sorry after him.

He loved the men and spent every hour of his time looking after them, and when we were having a fairly hot time in the trenches he would bring us up boxes of cigarettes and cheer us up. The men would do anything he asked them, and I am sure we will never get another padre like him. Everybody says that he has earned the V.C. many times over, and I can vouch for it myself from what I have seen him do many a time. He was asked not to go into action with the battalion, but he would not stop behind, and I am confident that no braver or holier man ever fell in battle than he.

---

29. Sergeant Flynn was with the 8th Royal Dublin Fusiliers.

Lieutenant Colonel H.R. Stirke[30], September 1917

He was one of the finest fellows I ever met, utterly fearless, always with a cheery word on his lips, and ever ready to go out and attend the wounded and dying under the heaviest fire. He was genuinely loved by everyone, and thoroughly deserved the unstinted praise he got from all ranks for his rare pluck and devotion to duty.

Sir Percival Phillips[31], Daily Express, August 1917

The Orangemen will not forget a certain Roman Catholic chaplain who lies in a soldier's grave in that sinister plain beyond Ypres. He went forward and back over the battle field with bullets whining about him, seeking out the dying and kneeling in the mud beside them to give them absolution, walking with death with a smile on his face, watched by his men with reverence and a kind of awe until a shell burst near him and he was killed. His familiar figure was seen and welcomed by hundreds of Irishmen who lay in that bloody place. Each time he came back across the field he was begged to remain in comparative safety. Smilingly he shook his head and went again into the storm. He had been with his boys at Ginchy and through other times of stress, and he would not desert them in their agony. They remember him as a saint – they speak his name with tears.

---

30. Temporary Officer Commanding, 8th Royal Dublin Fusiliers.
31. War correspondent.

Captain C.F. Healy[32], undated

If I had gone through the thousandth part of what Fr Doyle did, or if I had run a hundredth part of the risks he ran, I would have been dead long ago. Wherever there was danger, there was Fr Doyle; and wherever Fr Doyle was, there was danger … When shells were raining on us, he used to wander from dug-out to dug-out as if he were taking a walk for the good of his health. If a man was hit you would think he knew it by instinct; he was with the wounded man before anyone else was. It didn't matter where the man was lying, out he went to him.

Unnamed Belfast Orangeman[33], Glasgow Weekly News, September 1917

God never made a nobler soul … He didn't know the meaning of fear, and he didn't know what bigotry was. He was as ready to risk his life to take a drop of water to a wounded Ulsterman as to assist men of his own faith and regiment. If he risked his life to look after Ulster Protestant soldiers once, he did it a hundred times in the last few days. Father Doyle was a fine Christian in every sense of the word. He never tried to get things easy. He was always sharing the risks of

---

32. Royal Dublin Fusiliers. Captain Healy met with Fr Charles Doyle SJ some time after Fr Willie's death; this testimony is based on Charles Doyle's notes from that meeting.

33. This letter appeared anonymously.

the men, and had to be kept in restraint by the staff for his own protection. Many a time I have seen him walk beside a stretcher trying to console a wounded man, with bullets flying around him, and shells bursting every few yards.

Fr Frank Browne SJ, August 1917

All during these last months he was my greatest help, and to his saintly advice, and still more to his saintly example, I owe everything I felt and did. With him, as with others of us, his bravery was no mere physical show-off. He was afraid and felt fear deeply, how deeply few can realise. And yet the last word said of him to me by the adjutant of the Royal Irish Rifles in answer to my question, 'I hope you are taking care of Fr Doyle?', was, 'He is as fond of the shells as ever'. His one idea was to do God's work with the men, to make them saints. How he worked and how he prayed for this! Fine weather and foul he was always thinking of them and what he could do for them. In the cold winter he would not use the stove I bought for our dug-out. He scoffed at the idea as making it 'stuffy' – and that when the thermometer was fifteen to twenty degrees below zero, the coldest ever known in living memory here.

And how he loathed it all, the life and everything it implied! And yet nobody suspected it. God's will was his law. And to all who remonstrated, 'Must I not be about the Lord's business?' was his laughing answer in act and deed and not merely in word. May he rest in peace – it seems superfluous to pray for him.

Servant of God Monsignor Bernard Quinn[34]

Some time ago I read the *Life of Father William Doyle*, the Irish Jesuit-Chaplain, who was killed in the late World War. It was made up chiefly from a diary which he kept, and which, I am sure, he never intended for eyes other than his own. One day, not long ago, I met a Good Shepherd nun who had known Fr Doyle very intimately in Ireland. I asked her if she could tell me anything about the secret of his holiness. She told me that holiness was as natural to Fr Doyle as wings are to a bird. She had known him in his youth, and she had greeted him upon the occasion of his ordination. Like (Saint) Therese, he had always the desire of going on a foreign mission where he might suffer martyrdom.

He was never singular. In a gathering he was just one of his brethren, earnest in his work, and just as eager as the rest in his play. He practiced mortifications, but they were simple ones. For example, he ate everything

---

34. 1888-1940. He was born in New Jersey but both of his parents were Irish. He served as a chaplain in World War I but it seems unlikely that he met Fr Doyle while there, though he developed a devotion to him in later life, and had direct contact with people who knew him. Monsignor Quinn was renowned for his pastoral care of the African American community in Brooklyn and faced down violent opposition from the Ku Klux Klan. His cause for canonisation was opened in 2008.

at table just as it came from the kitchen. He refrained from using salt, and only when he was away from home did he take butter. This he did to avoid being noticed.

Unnamed Sister of Charity[35]

The first time I made a retreat under Fr Doyle was in 1911. He made a deep impression on us all. It was not eloquence which produced the effect, for he spoke very simply and homely, but something behind the words. One felt the man was speaking from his soul, pouring out the love of his heart for God … Between 1911 and his death I met Fr Doyle on several occasions and each time I was more and more impressed. He seemed more like an angel than a man. Zeal for souls and love of the Blessed Sacrament appeared to be the ruling passions of his life. As long as he could help a soul he cared not what trouble it cost him … When giving a retreat he would spend practically every spare moment in the chapel and to see him kneeling motionless before the tabernacle was a sermon in itself.

Unnamed Sister of Mercy

Father Doyle used occasionally to visit his sister who

---

35. This testimony, and the following from a Sister of Mercy, are both anonymous and were originally published by O'Rahilly in his biography. They presumably form part of the correspondence praising Fr Doyle that the Jesuits in general, and Fr Charles Doyle in particular, received following the death of Fr Willie.

was a nun in the Convent of Mercy, Cobh, of which I was also a member. Though I had seen him several times, it was not until his farewell visit for the front that I had my first interview with him …I said to him laughingly, 'For goodness' sake, Father, give me a blessing that will drive the spirit of tepidity out of me'. I knelt down and he gave me a long blessing and laid his hands on my head. I cannot describe what I felt but I rose from my knees dazed and as it were in a dream. I went straight to the chapel and there kneeling before the tabernacle I realised as never before that I was far from being a fervent religious, and with this realisation there came a great desire to become one. That blessing effected a greater change in my life than all the retreats I had made or spiritual helps I had received during my twenty years of religious life … It was as if, like his master, virtue went forth from him. He appeared to be in God's presence even when conversing with people on indifferent topics, while his childlike humility and utter absence of self were most striking and seemed to me to be the outcome of his union and all-absorbing love of God.